Dialectical Behavior Therapy for DID
The Workbook

ALSO BY JOHANNA KNYN

Multiplicity: Dissociative Identity Disorder

My Mommy Has Multiple Parts

Dialectical Behavior Therapy for DID
The Workbook

System-Affirming Skills, Mindfulness Practices,
and Emotional Regulation Exercises for People
with Dissociative Identities

JOHANNA "JOH" KNYN

North Atlantic Books
Huichin, unceded Ohlone land
Berkeley, California

Published by
North Atlantic Books
Huichin, unceded Ohlone land
Berkeley, California

Cover art © Irina Davydenko/Shutterstock.com
Cover design by Mimi Bark
Book design by Happenstance Type-O-Rama

Printed in Canada

Dialectical Behavior Therapy for DID—The Workbook: System-Affirming Skills, Mindfulness Practices, and Emotional Regulation Exercises for People with Dissociative Identities is sponsored and published by North Atlantic Books, an educational nonprofit based in the unceded Ohlone land Huichin (Berkeley, CA) that collaborates with partners to develop cross-cultural perspectives; nurture holistic views of art, science, the humanities, and healing; and seed personal and global transformation by publishing work on the relationship of body, spirit, and nature.

Disclaimer: This workbook is for general information purposes only. It does not consider the reader's specific needs, objectives, or circumstances; and it is not medical advice or a replacement for psychological therapy.

North Atlantic Books's publications are distributed to the US trade and internationally by Penguin Random House Publisher Services. For further information, visit our website at www.northatlanticbooks.com.

ISBN: 979-88-89842-41-5

1 2 3 4 5 6 7 8 9 MARQUIS 30 29 28 27 26 25

North Atlantic Books is committed to the protection of our environment. We print on recycled paper whenever possible and partner with printers who strive to use environmentally responsible practices.

CONTENTS

Welcome to
Your Workbook

Hi, I'm Johanna. I am a psychologist registered with the Australian Health Practitioner Regulation Agency (AHPRA). I work with Systems in Brisbane, Australia, in my private practice. I am passionate about developing resources that advocate for the empathetic and accurate understanding of those living with dissociative identities, like dissociative identity disorder (DID).

I believe everyone should have access to the tools that can assist in improving functionality and enhance their overall well-being. Dialectical behavior therapy (DBT) skills are particularly difficult to find in a System-friendly and affirming way. That's why the DBT skills in this workbook have been adapted to be more System-friendly and affirming.

DBT was founded in the 1970s by Dr. Marsha Linehan, originally for those living with borderline personality disorder (BPD). DBT skills can be helpful for a variety of other conditions beyond BPD. The overall goal of DBT skills is to help with changing behaviors, thinking, and interpersonal patterns associated with problems in life. It can also help with emotional regulation. This workbook is designed as an adapted version of the skills within DBT, for those who experience multiplicity of self.

For transparency, I am a singlet or singleton. What that means is, I am not a System or someone living with dissociative identities. I acknowledge that although I have the privilege of working every day with folks living with DID, I do not have lived experience as a System. As such, active steps were taken to involve voices from the DID community prior to the publication of this workbook. It is imperative that all materials designed to assist any group has had members of that group consulted in the development of those materials. Lived-experience voices matter.

How to Use
Your Workbook

This is your book to use how you choose. If you want to avoid certain pages to start, as they may be too distressing for you—that's OK. If you want to make notes all over the pages to help apply things to your System—awesome! This workbook is for *all* of you.

Secondly, while you are strongly encouraged to practice the skills discussed in this workbook, we understand that a healing journey is not linear or formulaic and that each Headmate, or alter—short for alternate state consciousness—is most likely at a different stage of their own healing. We also acknowledge that each Headmate has different abilities. For example, a Headmate that is five years old internally would exhibit behaviors, skills, and abilities that align with someone in that age group.

If you feel uncomfortable about any skill or don't feel like you're in the right headspace to do the skill, stop or skip it. You are the expert in you. Trust yourself, your intuitive knowing, and the wisdom of your System. Skills-building starts with knowledge, developing an understanding of what's what. You are welcome to start this workbook simply by reading the content, then coming back a second, third, or umpteenth time to begin practicing the skills you've read about.

Also, before practicing a skill, even if it isn't the first time, check in with your Headmates and ask the following:

- Capacity check
  - Do we have the energy to do this right now? Do we have enough energy to practice this skill or a new skill? Do we have the capacity?

- Choice check
  - Do I want to do this skill right now? Is there any internal resistance about practicing a new skill or this skill?
  - It is also important to know that not everyone internally may want to have their details recorded in this workbook. That's OK. Just because a worksheet asks for a Headmate's name doesn't mean it has to be written down. No one has to engage with the content if they don't want to.
  - Every Headmate can choose to engage with the content. It's important to recognize and acknowledge each other's choice.
  - There is no part of this workbook that requires the sharing of your history or past experiences. This workbook is designed to build skills, adapted from DBT, to be used in the here and now.

Lastly, language is important. It helps us understand each other and communicate important messages. Within this workbook, specific terms are used. I acknowledge that within the multiplicity community, like all communities, there is a variety of ways things can be described. For those new to using affirming language, a dictionary of the terms used in this workbook and in the community can be found toward the end of workbook. Should there be terms that do not resonate with your System, you are more than welcome to cross them out and write the terms *you* use.

LET'S BEGIN . . .

Orientation and Key Concepts

- Setting Our Intentions
- Our Window of Tolerance
- Safe Versus Safe Enough

SETTING OUR INTENTIONS

Before getting started with the modules, let's begin by taking a moment and identifying your intentions for using this workbook. Unlike a goal, which is specific, time bound, and measurable, you are encouraged to set intentions for this workbook. Think of a goal as the end point and your intentions as the journey itself. For example, your goal for this workbook may be to complete all the worksheets, while your intention may be to engage with the workbook in a mindful and present way.

_____

_____

_____

_____

_____

_____

_____

_____

_____

_____

WORKSHEET 1

Below is some space to write your intentions. If you are having a hard time thinking of what to put down, review the examples below. We understand that there may be only one or two intentions, depending on how many of you are choosing to actively engage with this workbook. If you need more space to write, there is extra space at the back of this book, or you can use the alternate space on the Worksheet 2 that may be more System-friendly.

EXAMPLES

- We intend to have an open mind-set when engaging with the content and worksheets. We are willing to try out new things.
- We intend to actively engage with this workbook. When we open our workbook, we make the choice to be as grounded as we can to mindfully engage with the content.
- We will practice gratitude. As we notice things come up for us and other Headmates, we will acknowledge them and practice gratitude for them in doing this workbook.
- We will set boundaries with ourselves. When we hear others inside being clear with "No," "We are not ready for this content right now," "We need to take a break"—we will choose to listen and honor those boundaries.
- We will be ourselves. When engaging with our workbook, we know that it is ours and that we do not have to mask our answers. No one will have access to our workbook unless we choose to share it.
- We will speak kindly to ourselves. If we notice someone inside is having a tough time with the workbook content, we will choose to be patient and kind with them. We acknowledge everyone is at a different stage of their own healing journey.

Our intentions for this workbook are:

_____

_____

_____

_____

_____

_____

_____

_____

_____

_____

_____

_____

_____

WORKSHEET 2

This worksheet shows an alternate way that your System can note down your intentions.

Headmate 1

My intentions for this workbook are:

_____

_____

Headmate 2

My intentions for this workbook are:

_____

_____

Headmate 3

My intentions for this workbook are:

_____

_____

Headmate 4

My intentions for this workbook are:

_____

_____

THE WINDOW OF TOLERANCE

HYPERAROUSAL

You feel angry, anxious, overhwhelmed, and/or out of control. This is a *mobilisation* response to a thread. The body wants to fight or flee (run away).

WIDENING YOUR WINDOW

Working with your therapist can help you learn and practice the skills to widen your Window of Tolerance. Your therapist can help you do this at the right pace for you to learn what works specifically for you and your System.

WINDOW OF TOLERANCE

This is where the body feels just right. You are alert but not anxious, and calm but not tired. You are in the rest-and-digest zone. Your body feels safe, or safe enough.

STRESS AND TRAUMA

Stress and trauma can make your window smaller, meaning you are more likely to exit your window more quickly. With a small window, you may be seen to react over small things.

HYPOAROUSAL

You feel zoned out, numb, and disconnected from your body, your emotions, and the world around you. Time can go missing. This is an *immobilization* response to threat. The body wants to freeze, fawn, or flop.

Figure 1.1.

OUR WINDOW OF TOLERANCE

This is one of the most important parts of the workbook. You are encouraged to complete a check-in every time you open your workbook. This check-in is to determine whether you are in your Window of Tolerance and can safely engage with the content.

Window of Tolerance is a term used to describe the optimal zone we as humans can exist in, to best function and thrive in everyday life, versus being in survival mode. Part of working toward Functional Multiplicity is widening your Window of Tolerance. Functional Multiplicity is part of the recovery process where your System works toward establishing strong and healthy relationships with each other, while Headmates maintain their individuality within the System. These relationships are built on respect and cooperation, developing a sense of internal community and collaboration.

When we are in our window, we have access to our prefrontal cortex. This is the part of your brain that sits behind your forehead. What we mean by "access" is that this part of the brain is online. When the prefrontal cortex is online, our executive functioning skills are also in working order. Such skills include:

- organizing
- planning and prioritizing complex tasks
- starting actions and projects and staying focused on them to completion
- regulating emotions
- practicing self-control
- practicing good time management
- decision-making

Having access to your executive functions will equip you to work with the content of this workbook, align with your intentions, and help you be as grounded as possible.

SYSTEM-FRIENDLY TIPS

We assume Functional Multiplicity as the preferred goal for wellness. We acknowledge that not all Systems have this goal and that Final or Complete Fusion may also desired. However, this workbook is designed with System-affirming care in mind.

CHECK-IN EXERCISE

Read the words below. Check those that apply to you in what you are noticing in this moment, as you read. You can do this exercise every time before engaging with your workbook.

HYPERAROUSAL

- ✓ increased heart rate
- ✓ quicker and shallower breathing
- ✓ tunnel vision, or vision becoming sharper
- ✓ dry mouth
- ✓ tense muscles
- ✓ sweaty palms
- ✓ racing thoughts
- ✓ dizziness or lightheadedness
- ✓ butterflies in the stomach

HYPOAROUSAL

- ✓ feelings of paralysis
- ✓ shallow breathing
- ✓ feeling emotionally numb or empty
- ✓ lacking motivation
- ✓ wanting to socially withdraw
- ✓ difficulty making decisions
- ✓ feelings of hopelessness
- ✓ inability to focus and concentrate
- ✓ a sense of disconnection from the body
- ✓ a sense of disconnection from your feelings or emotions
- ✓ brain fog
- ✓ exhaustion and fatigue

IN OUR WINDOW OF TOLERANCE

- ✓ feeling emotionally flexible: I can experience different emotions without getting stuck or feeling consumed by them
- ✓ feeling present in the moment
- ✓ feeling sociable, within my own natural limits of sociability
- ✓ feeling generally safe enough within my world

SYSTEM-FRIENDLY TIPS

Each Headmate may have a preferred state they enter into when protecting themselves and the System. We can consider this their autopilot response. Consider identifying Headmate preferences or autopilot responses.

CHECK-IN EXERCISE

This exercise can help you develop your grounding skills. Knowing what you are trying to feel less of, hyper- or hypoaroused, is great, but knowing what you are trying to feel more of is even better.

Knowing what being grounded feels like is helpful. Understanding what being grounded feels like from experience is our ultimate goal. Developing familiarity with it helps you to be able to recognize more easily, "Oh, we are out of our Window of Tolerance," and as such, practice your skills to return to it. It can also help build familiarity of, "So this is what being grounded feels like," so you don't miss it when it happens.

Try writing a few things down. Try to include what the body may experience, what the internal world may feel like, or what it may be like emotionally or socially for you.

When we are in our Window of Tolerance, we typically experience:

_____

_____

_____

_____

_____

_____

SYSTEM-FRIENDLY TIPS

It can be difficult at first to know what being grounded actually feels like. Your nervous system is used to being in a hyper- or hypoaroused state, so be patient and compassionate with yourselves. This is a journey. No one wins the gold medal on their first attempt.

WORKSHEET 3

Let's start collecting some data about your System and the autopilot responses of some of your Headmates. This can help better identify who may be fronting, when a Headmate has control over the body, or close to front at any point in time, especially when dysregulated. It can also help, when working with that Headmate or yourself, to do what you may be able to do to return to a Window of Tolerance and feel grounded.

Circle the Headmates' or your preference or autopilot response.

Headmate Name:

Hyperarousal

flight   fight

Hypoarousal

freeze   fawn   flop

Calm or within our Window of Tolerance

Comments:

_____

_____

_____

Headmate Name:

Hyperarousal

flight   fight

Hypoarousal

freeze   fawn   flop

Calm or within our Window of Tolerance

Comments:

_____

_____

_____

Headmate Name:

Hyperarousal

flight   fight

Hypoarousal

freeze   fawn   flop

Calm or within our Window of Tolerance

Comments:

_____

_____

_____

WORKSHEET 3 EXAMPLE

Below is an example of how the worksheet can be filled out. Again, should you not want your name written down, you can choose an alias or another anchor point to help others in the System better understand you, while also respecting your personal boundary of not wanting to be known just yet.

Headmate Name: Felix

Hyperarousal

flight   fight

Hypoarousal

freeze   fawn   flop

Calm or within our Window of Tolerance

Comments: Felix is a physical protector. When we feel ungrounded, not safe enough, he will front to make sure we are protected. When he is fronting or close to front, the muscles tense up, the body feels hot and sweaty, and the teeth are clenched.

Headmate Name: "The Silent One"

Hyperarousal

flight   fight

Hypoarousal

freeze   fawn   flop

Calm or within our Window of Tolerance

Comments: The Silent One is a protector. We don't know much about them. We know that when they are close to front, it feels like we can't move the body. Like it is frozen in place. The eyes feel very wide, like we can't or shouldn't blink. The breath rate slows down and it's hard to think, or the Headspace feels foggy. It sometimes feels like when the Silent One is fronting, no one else is allowed up front.

SAFE VERSUS SAFE ENOUGH

You may have read or heard a lot about working toward feeling safe. This is an especially major theme when you are in therapy and have experienced trauma. In this workbook, we acknowledge that at first, and perhaps for a long time, feeling "safe" doesn't feel safe.

The idea of safety can be reconsidered as more a spectrum of safety rather than a binary concept that has only two possible options. As we reconsider safety to be more a spectrum, try marking on the spectrum below to indicate where you believe "safe enough" belongs—the cutoff point, let's say.

An arrow has been placed on the spectrum as guide to where "safe enough" typically belongs, at least over the halfway point.

Figure 1.2. The safe versus unsafe spectrum

THE ALL-OR-NOTHING VIEW OF SAFETY

SAFE *100%*

UNSAFE *0%*

Figure 1.3. The all-or-nothing view of safety

Figure 1.3 shows the all-or-nothing or binary way of understanding the concept of safety. When we engage in all-or-nothing thinking, we create two options, and only two options—this or that. We ignore or can't see that there is actually a lot of gray or nuance to things.

This way of thinking makes total sense for a traumatized brain. There is nothing wrong or broken with your brain because it thinks about things this way. It actually kept you safe for a very long time (see the System-Friendly Tip). Your brain wants things to be simple; it's either this or that. This has helped your brain make quick decisions to protect itself and stay alive. It is normal for our brains to do this when we are presented with a threat or are in a threatening environment.

With this all-or-nothing thinking, you are either safe (100 percent) or unsafe (0 percent safe). When you really think about it, 100 percent safe isn't a real thing. Can anyone or anything in this world truly be 100 percent safe? We don't think so. We do believe, however, that there are things and people that can be 100 percent unsafe (0 percent safe).

If we continue to rely on this all-or-nothing thinking, it means that there will always be only unsafety (0 percent safe), because 100 percent safe is unrealistic. So we redefine safety as a spectrum because that's more realistic.

SYSTEM-FRIENDLY TIPS

When we mention "safe" here, we acknowledge that this does not mean the absence of unpleasantness. We simply mean that this way of thinking kept you alive.

We also acknowledge that your reality, and anyone's reality, is constructed by our experiences with the world. We acknowledge the significant number of experiences of unsafety you and your System has likely endured. We are in no way suggesting that your past experiences are not real.

THE SAFETY SPECTRUM: SAFE ENOUGH

The box in Figure 1.4 can be used to describe in more detail where "safe enough" likely lives.

Anywhere between the box and "Safe—100 percent" is unrealistic for pretty much any relationship and the world around us, but feeling 98 percent may be attainable over a long period of time with lots of consistent evidence within the relationship or environment.

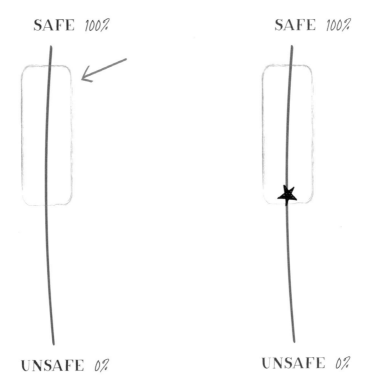

Figure 1.4. The safety spectrum

Figure 1.5. The safety spectrum: safe enough

If your relationships or environment enter anywhere between the box and "Unsafe—0 percent," this signals an unhealthy and dysfunctional space. Things in this space likely need ending, or you need to leave.

As this workbook is for folks with DID or the lived experience of multiplicity, who have most likely experienced repeated relational trauma and traumatic environments created or maintained by people, we will use relationships with people for our example here.

Healthy relationships start at the star in figure 1.5, right where enough safety is established to continue engaging with the person and the relationship. As the relationship develops with an acquaintance or friend, the star moves farther into the box and closer to "Safe—100 percent." With each interaction where you feel respected, heard, validated, and other traits that build a sense of safety for you, the star moves up a little bit.

As the star moves, it shows us that we are building more trust and a sense that "this person is safe enough to continue the relationship." When something happens in a relationship that hurts our feelings, where we might feel rejected, triggered, or something else—the star moves back down a little. This can be a helpful visual when thinking about your relationships and where each person in your life sits on the spectrum of safety at any point in time.

This can be especially helpful when we have our feelings hurt or are out of our Window of Tolerance. Remember that when you are out of your Window, your prefrontal cortex is not online, and you are at risk of making impulsive decisions such as ending relationships immediately that may actually still remain in the "safe enough" box. Using this visual, we can see that although the star has moved down, it may not have moved out of the "safe enough" box.

There are, of course, nonnegotiable behaviors that others can do that simply bump them right out of the safe enough box all together. There is more on this in the "Setting Boundaries" module below. If your boundaries are being respected, this is also a good indicator that safety is being developed in your relationships.

WORKSHEET 4

Using figure 1.6, place an X or dots on the line. Reflect on where those in your life sit on the spectrum of safety. An example is in gray.

SAFE *100%*

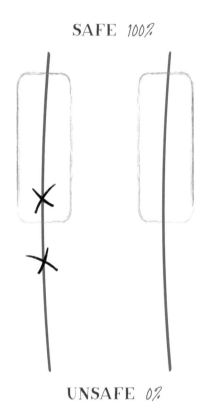

UNSAFE *0%*

Figure 1.6. The safety spectrum: safe enough

Example: My new therapist or counselor is "safe enough" for:

  1. me to attend therapy, and

  2. talk about some of my Headmates or Parts, but not safe enough yet to talk about my relationship with my family or our past.

WORKBOOK MODULES OVERVIEW

These are the skills you will be learning within this workbook. They can be completed at your own pace, by yourselves or with your treating professional.

Grounding Skills

In DBT, this is called Mindfulness Skills.

Managing Our Emotions Skills

In DBT, this is called Emotion Regulation Skills.

Values-Guided Action Skills

This is a bonus module.

People and Parts Relationship Skills

In DBT, this is called Interpersonal Effectiveness Skills.

Surviving the Moment Core Skills

In DBT, this is called Distress Tolerance Skills.

Grounding Skills

- Connecting with the Present
- Pain, Damage, Illness
- Accepting My Internal Experience
- Understanding Our Behavior

CONNECTING WITH THE PRESENT

Being grounded in the present moment is a foundational skill. It is an essential skill for all Systems. When we are grounded, we are oriented to present reality: the now. We can connect with the body, as it is now. We know where we are. We know what the date is. We are hooked in to the present.

When we are dissociated, we are in an in-between place: not really here, in the now; not really anywhere. Dissociation isn't always unhelpful. You are encouraged to discuss dissociation and how you experience it with your therapist, if you have one, to learn when it has been functional for your System and where it may no longer be helpful.

When we are ungrounded, floaty, dissociated, this can lead to a greater risk of flashbacks. Flashbacks are a vivid experience in which aspects of a traumatic event are relived as opposed to remembered; it feels as if the traumatic event is happening right now. This is why grounding is so important to help you and the System stay here, in the now, where those things are not happening anymore.

> **Notice:** Notice your surroundings. This is where we use our five senses exercise to hook into the present moment.
>
> **Describe:** To further ground to the present, use as much detail to describe what is being noticed.
>
> **Listen:** Using your ears and your heart, listen to what comes up for you. This includes external and internal noise.
>
> **Breathe:** Use the power of the breath to connect with the present moment.

Before we begin "Connecting with the Present" exercises, let's first ensure that the environment where we are doing these exercises is comfortable and feels "safe enough" to you.

We acknowledge that it is not uncommon for Systems to also experience co-occurring neurodivergence like autism (ASD) or attention deficit hyperactivity disorder (ADHD). As such, we also want to ensure that you are accommodating your environment for your sensory needs.

As you assess your environment and decide the best place to be for the "Connecting with the Present" exercises, if the location is outside your home, we encourage you to save it in your maps app. Saving it will allow all Headmates to know the location of this "safe enough" place for connecting with the present moment. It can also be shared with support persons if you feel comfortable doing so.

Let's get into the worksheet for creating a comfortable environment to practice your grounding skills. Of course, you can have multiple spaces; let's start with identifying one first. Here are some questions to ask about the environment when the environment is your own home.

Is the room private? This can be important for you to feel comfortable enough to really hook into the present moment and not worry in the back of your mind that you are being observed, perceived, or judged by others in the space.

Is the space free from distraction? Having your phone ding when you are partway through the exercise can be jarring and take you away from the intention of the exercise.

Is the space free from potential triggers? When you are connecting with the present moment through noticing what is around you, we want to ensure that there isn't anything around you that may trigger you or someone else in the System. The intention is to connect to the present moment, not with moments from the past. We want to reduce the risk of flashbacks wherever we can.

Is it sensory friendly? This includes all your senses—connecting with the present moment uses all the senses. If the environment is not sensory-friendly, we run the risk of meltdown or shutdown states that can also lead into flashbacks. Think about: Is the space too loud? Is the space too quiet? Is the space too hot or cold? Is the space cozy enough for us? Is the space too bright? Is there a funky smell in the space?

Is it comfortable? Also, think about the body itself. Will it be seated in a comfortable position? If I sit for a while, will it hurt my body?

SYSTEM-FRIENDLY TIPS

For many Systems, co-occurring physical disabilities and impairments can also be present. Be mindful of your physical health and how you can adjust yourself or accommodate for your physical capacity.

Here are some questions to ask about the environment when the environment is the community, for example in a park.

Is the space private? As before, we want you to feel comfortable to engage in connecting with the present moment, not worried that others are staring at you.

Is the space free from potential triggers? Again, we want to ensure that there isn't anything around you that may trigger you or someone else in the System. The intention is to connect to the present moment, not with moments from the past. If you are unsure, you are encouraged to ask inside, "Is this an OK space to try our grounding skills?" Listen for a strong "No" or a strong feeling of resistance.

Is it sensory-friendly? This includes all your senses—connecting with the present moment uses all the senses. If the environment is not sensory-friendly, we run the risk of meltdown or shutdown states that could also lead into flashbacks. Think about: Is the space too loud? Is the space too quiet? Is the space too hot or cold? Is the space cozy enough for us? Is the space too bright? Is there a funky smell in the space?

Is it comfortable? Also think about the body itself. Will it be seated in a comfortable position?

WORKSHEET 5

What is the location of our comfortable space for practicing our grounding skills:

- Inside the house

  What room:

  _____

- Outside in the community

  The address:

  _____

What steps do I need to take to ensure we are free from distraction or are in private? For example:

- Put our phone in airplane mode
- Put a note on our door saying "Do Not Disturb for *x* Minutes: Grounding in Progress"
- Have a water bottle next to us and a small snack
- Wear headphones to let others know not to disturb me

  _____

  _____

  _____

  _____

Is the space sensory-friendly?

- The brightness is just right: not too bright or too dark
- There are no annoying or distracting sounds
- The body will feel **OK** seated, standing, etc., in this position for at least five minutes
- We have something to fidget with if needed
- There are no weird, funky, or overpowering smells around

Is the space as free from triggers as possible?

- Yes
- No—but we can do the following to make it so: remove toys, face a different direction, only go at certain times

_____

_____

_____

Now to the exercises.

WORKSHEET 6

As you sit down, ready to engage in the grounding exercises to come, take a moment to settle into the environment that you've chosen. Ideally you are now comfortable to start the grounding exercises. If not, go back and reassess— just because it was comfortable yesterday doesn't mean it will be today. You can't be expected to feel grounded and safe enough in an environment that is uncomfortable.

Before starting the grounding exercises below, we want to invite others in the Headspace to join and take part. In adapting DBT skills for multiplicity, we encourage you to take a moment prior to any exercise or worksheet to invite your other Headmates to join you.

Step 1: We encourage you to take this moment, now that you are settled into your environment, to connect with the Headspace. Take a slow breath in and out through the nose. This slow breath will be used as our cue to the body and Headspace that you are about to begin this exercise. You can either close your eyes or look into your lap or downward. Here we are reducing the external stimulus to give you the best chance for the message to be sent to the others inside.

Step 2: Either say aloud or think loudly inside the Headspace: "We are going to practice our grounding skills. Anyone who would like to join me is welcome. We are in [describe your location a little]." Describing your location in a little detail may help those inside build familiarity with the space.

Step 3: Pause for a moment and allow the message to be received by the others inside. Take another slow breath in and out through the nose. This is another physiological cue to indicate that the grounding exercise is about to begin.

Step 4: Now you are ready to complete your grounding exercise. You can choose to try all or only some of it.

Remember that this is your journey and you are free to engage in the exercises at your own pace. We do encourage you to give each a try first and then determine which you are ready for at this stage of your healing journey and which you may need more time or capacity for.

WORKSHEET 7

Notice your surroundings. Just observe them; the next worksheet is where you can describe your surroundings. Use your senses to ground and connect with the present moment. Find a space where you feel comfortable to complete this exercise.

Using your eyes, what can you see? Look around the room, the space you are in, and simply notice what catches your eye. Is anything colorful or strangely shaped?

Using your ears, what can you hear? Notice the sounds happening around you, externally. Are birds chirping? Are cars driving by?

If it feels comfortable, move your tongue around your mouth. Can you notice any flavors? What texture is the inside of your cheek?

Notice the pressure of the seat against your body. Notice the air on your skin. Begin to be aware of your body.

Begin to breathe slowly and intentionally. Are there any smells around? Essential oils can be a powerful grounding tool when they are pleasant. Maybe light a candle.

How is your body moving? Simply notice the movement as you walk around the space you are in. Notice how your legs move as you put one in front of the other.

Take a look around the space you are in. Notice how far you are from other objects, and how close. Bring awareness to the distance you are from other things.

WORKSHEET 8

To further ground to the present, use as much detail as possible to describe what you are noticing. Write down a few things about what you noticed when connecting with your senses.

_____

_____

_____

_____

_____

_____

_____

_____

_____

_____

_____

_____

_____

WORKSHEET 9

Using your ears and your heartbeat, listen to what comes up for you. This is where we begin to notice the difference between external and internal noise.

Listening with your ears, tune in to the noise happening outside. Are there cars going by, birds chirping, or the hum of an appliance? Bring your awareness to the external noise. This can be challenging, so take your time. Stop whenever you need to. This exercise is aimed at providing an invitation for connection with your Headmates.

Tune in to your internal noise. This can look like listening to what is happening inside. It could be auditory in sounds like thoughts or chatter; it could be a feeling or an emotion that seems distant; it could be a sense of knowing something.

To finish this exercise, you can say aloud or think inside, "Thank you," and take a deep breath in through your nose, making a small "ah" sound as you exhale. This can help acknowledge your Headmates and signal the end of the exercise.

SYSTEM-FRIENDLY TIPS

Tuning in to your internal noise is not designed to encourage memory sharing or trauma sharing. That type of sharing is to be done in the safety of therapy.

WORKSHEET 10: BREATHE

Use the power of the breath to connect with the body in the present moment.

Start by settling into a comfortable position and allow your eyes to soften (you don't need to close them).

Begin by taking several long, slow deep breaths, breathing in fully and exhaling fully. The depth is whatever feels most comfortable to you. There is no need to push yourself. It is not about getting lots of air in, but about connecting with the breath.

Breathe in through your nose and out through your mouth. Allow your breath to find its own natural rhythm. Bring your attention to each in-breath as it comes in through your nostrils, travels down into your lungs, and makes the belly expand.

Now notice each out-breath as your belly contracts and air moves up through your lungs and back up through the nostrils or mouth.

Use the power of the breath to connect with the body in the present moment.

Notice how the sensation of the inhale is different from the exhale. The air may feel cool as it enters through the nose and warm as you exhale.

Simply breathe as you would normally, not striving to change anything about the breath.

Don't try to control your breath in any way. Observe and accept this experience in this moment without judgment, paying attention to each inhale and exhale. If you prefer, try looking online for guided breathing exercises. These can help practice bringing attention to your breathing while having another voice guide you through the process.

SYSTEM-FRIENDLY TIPS

If this exercise is too overwhelming for you at the moment, that's OK. Let's start with something gentler. Rather than changing your breath, let's just notice the breath. If that is too difficult, that's OK too. This may not be the exercise for you.

PAIN, DAMAGE, ILLNESS

WHY

As a System, it can get rather confusing when we think about our connection to the body. Most Systems, in my experience, have a really hard time connecting to the body—it is often viewed as an unsafe place to be. Honestly, that makes sense, but it can become unhelpful when the body isn't doing well. So, the "Pain, Damage, Illness" concept and worksheet were developed. It is a simple way of assessing the body and its wellness in the present moment. It is designed to assist in determining what course of action to take. It is not to be used as a replacement for therapy and your general health practitioner. We remind you to pace yourself as you go through the workbook and make sure you are grounded enough to engage with the content.

As a System you can experience all three, two, or just one. For example, you can be in pain without the body being damaged or ill, or the body could be ill and be dissociated from the pain. It is important to assess the body accurately in order to make the best decision to stay well.

PAIN

When we talk about pain, and the experience of pain only, separate from and without damage or illness, we are talking about somatic flashbacks, pain reexperienced in the body as a result of a past traumatic events. We can also label it as past pain being experienced in the here and now. It is important to understand this, as it will inform how you treat it. You are encouraged to work with your therapist, counselor, or mental health professional specifically to learn more about your experience with somatic flashbacks.

DAMAGE

When we talk about the body being damaged, what we are referring to is typically bruising, broken bones, cuts, burns, sprains, strains, and this list goes on. We can understand damage as "the body is hurt" in the present. If we are accident-prone or damage our body often, make time regularly to check the body for damage.

ILLNESS

When we talk about illness, we are referring to things like a sore throat, chest infection, flu or cold, stomachache, diarrhea, a urinary tract infection, fever, and so on. We separate illness and damage because the course of treatment will likely be different. Illness is also something experienced in the present.

SOMATIC FLASHBACKS

Somatic flashbacks are experienced as physical sensations, pain, or discomfort in areas of the body that were affected by the trauma. There are no limits to where in the body these can be experienced; any part of the body can be involved.

This pain, sensation, or discomfort cannot be explained by any other health issues, meaning it is not explained by present-day damage, illness, or as an ongoing issue from past damage, such as a bone healing incorrectly or nerve damage.

Somatic flashbacks, like all flashbacks, can be triggered by anything. There is no restriction to what your triggers may be. There is more about how you may be able to help your System when experiencing somatic flashbacks in the next sections.

WORKSHEET 11

Where am I experiencing this? Use the sketch of the physical body to color in the location you may be experiencing pain or have damage or illness. An example is on page 41.

SYSTEM-FRIENDLY TIPS

You can bring this along to your doctor's appointment if this helps communicate your experiences. You can also put the date on it to help remember when you experienced these things.

WORKSHEET 11 EXAMPLE

Here's an example of what it may look like for you.

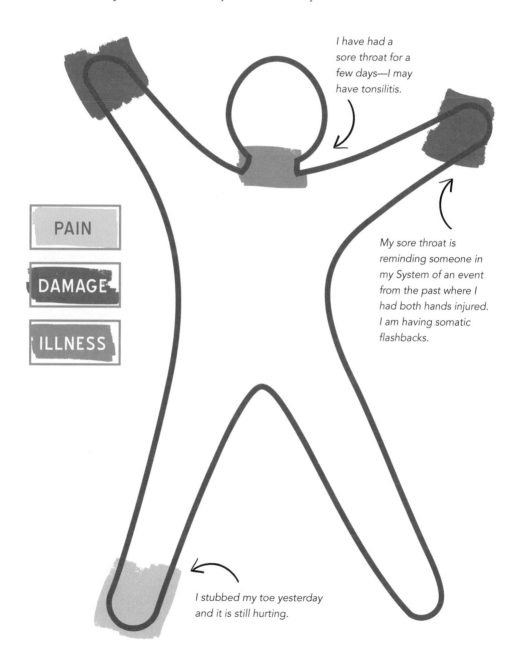

I have had a sore throat for a few days—I may have tonsilitis.

My sore throat is reminding someone in my System of an event from the past where I had both hands injured. I am having somatic flashbacks.

PAIN

DAMAGE

ILLNESS

I stubbed my toe yesterday and it is still hurting.

WORKSHEET 11

Where am I experiencing this? Use the sketch of the physical body to color in the location you may be experiencing pain or have damage or illness.

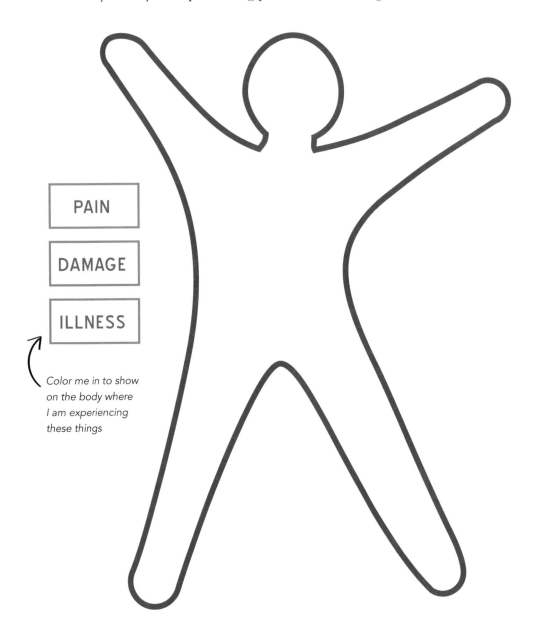

PAIN

DAMAGE

ILLNESS

Color me in to show on the body where I am experiencing these things

WORKSHEET 11 EXTRA COPY

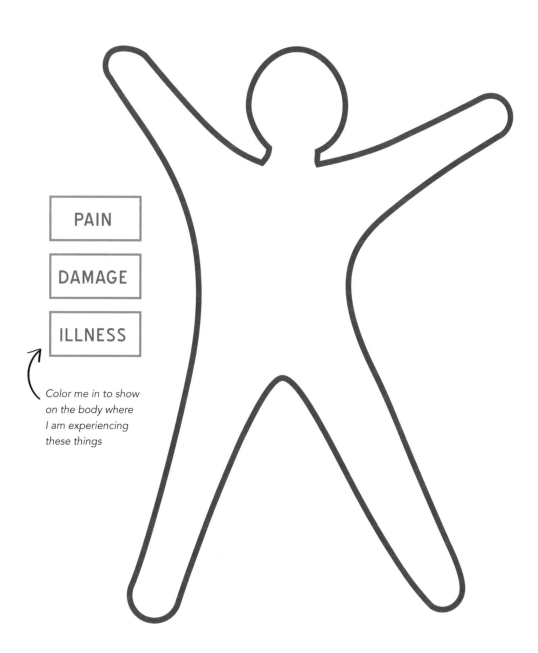

PAIN

DAMAGE

ILLNESS

*Color me in to show
on the body where
I am experiencing
these things*

Once you have determined what is happening for the body—all, some, or just one of these experiences—we can then determine the best course of action to treat the body.

PAIN

When we are experiencing somatic flashbacks—only pain—we then need to work on assisting the Headmates to orient to the present. I strongly encourage you to work with your treating therapist to learn in more detail how to do this and to be supported through this part of your journey.

DAMAGE

When the body is damaged, first we need to determine what the damage is and where. Once identified, we can treat it. For example, apply antiseptic and a bandage to a cut. We also need to determine whether we need to see a doctor to address the damage. When in doubt, see your doctor.

ILLNESS

When we are ill, this is when we need to determine whether we need medical attention or not. For example, is my sore throat something that will pass with rest, or do I need antibiotics? It is best to be cautious and see your doctor.

MORE ABOUT SOMATIC FLASHBACKS

When we are experiencing somatic flashbacks—only pain—we then need to work on assisting the Headmates who are triggered to orient to the present moment. What may be happening when a Headmate is experiencing a somatic flashback:

1. The fronting Headmate could be experiencing the somatic flashback, leading to the body experiencing the pain.

2. A Headmate in the back could be experiencing a somatic flashback, and the body feels the passive influence of those body sensations: the pain.

Passive influence can be described as intrusions from Headmates that are not currently prominent in the mind or using the body, otherwise known as fronting, and they can vary in strength and level of influence.

I strongly encourage you to work with your treating therapist, if you have one, to learn in more detail how to do this and to be supported through this part of your journey.

SYSTEM-FRIENDLY TIPS

You can visit the Dissociative Identity Disorder Research (DIDR) website for more evidence-based information: https://did-research.org.

What may help you and your fellow Headmates when experiencing somatic flashbacks: Practice the "Connecting with the Present" exercise, but skip all elements that involve the body. This may look like connecting with the sounds around you, a specific song that helps you connect with the current year, or using a fidget object to help engage with texture or movement that is technically body-related but more about connecting with what the body is touching rather than the body itself.

If you are experiencing somatic flashbacks from passive influence, or someone inside is experiencing them but the fronting Headmate is not, you can use your voice externally (saying things out loud) and your inner voice (talking to those in the Headspace) to orient them to the present moment.

This can be as simple as saying, "It is 2025. We are not back there. I am here for you. You are not alone. The body is experiencing a body memory. We are not currently being harmed."

You can, of course, create your own version of the example above. Ensure you are grounding into the date (at least the year), that the body is not being hurt or harmed, and that they are not alone—they have you and other Headmates and other external supports. We want them to know what *is* happening and what *is not* happening.

SYSTEM-FRIENDLY TIPS

Those new to the language used in this workbook are reminded of the "Commonly Used Terms" list at the back of the book to refer to throughout your reading journey.

ACCEPTING MY INTERNAL EXPERIENCE

WHY

Learning to accept your internal experience is essential in working toward Functional Multiplicity. When we look at the traditional DBT skills, we refer to Radical Acceptance, which is about recognizing that some parts of life are beyond our control, and that struggling against them, resisting them, or denying them leads to further suffering. Radical Acceptance involves the process of recognizing reality and making peace with it and the things that cannot be changed, such as being multiple and part of a System.

When we are affected by intense experiences that we may not be able to explain or make sense of, our natural reaction may be anger, fear, guilt, or even shame. These reactions are normal and valid.

When we are totally unaware of why we are experiencing something, it may indicate that our connections or relationships with the rest of our System have not yet developed into the trusting internal community that we seek on the journey toward wellness, however you define that for yourselves. That's OK—it is a journey; your unique journey.

Acceptance simply means accepting our current reality and letting go of control to find out the why. Think of it as allowing the experience to occur. Better understanding of why things are happening is something you can do when you are in your Window of Tolerance and clearer of mind to discover the answers.

This can be a challenging exercise. Are you in your Window of Tolerance to continue? As a System, you experience both the external world and your own internal world differently to singlets. The internal world is the place your Headmates reside. We can also call this the Headspace. Everyone's internal worlds are unique and can be experienced in different ways.

SYSTEM-FRIENDLY TIPS

We assume Functional Multiplicity as the preferred goal for wellness. We acknowledge that not all Systems have this goal and that Final Fusion or Complete Fusion may also be desired. However, this workbook is designed with System-affirming care in mind.

Some Systems have a rich, complex, and visual internal world, while some have no visual elements to theirs. There is no "right" or "better" internal world. Each Headmate themselves is likely to experience the internal world differently from the others—that's normal.

Part of the grounding work as a System is accepting that your internal experience is valid, OK, and right where it needs to be at this moment. This can be simple but difficult. Accepting multiplicity takes time, compassion for the self and your Headmates, and consistent work. Acceptance is not knowing everything about what happens inside and why. It is simply about the willingness to tolerate the reality. It is also about noticing without judgment or an attempt to control everything. This is the harder part.

WHY IS IT IMPORTANT TO ACCEPT MY INTERNAL EXPERIENCE?

Rejecting or denying the reality of your internal experience does not change the reality. Changing reality, the way you experience your internal world and your internal community, first requires accepting reality. Emotional pain cannot be avoided, not in the long run. Sure, with dissociation it can be avoided. But that doesn't mean it goes away. Pain is a signal, communicating to us that something is not quite right. Rejecting your reality only prolongs the suffering.

Refusing to accept reality can keep you stuck in unhappiness, bitterness, anger, confusion, sadness, shame, or other painful emotions. It can also create more internal chaos. Rejecting or denying your internal experience can send the message to your Headmates that they are rejected and denied. This leads to increased chaos internally and more suffering.

The path out of chaos is *through* the suffering, not around it or over it. Accepting the suffering is part of climbing out of the chaos.

SYSTEM-FRIENDLY TIPS

Acceptance does not, in any way, mean we agree with or approve of what happened to us. It does not mean the person is off the hook. It simply means you are accepting that the past happened. It also does not mean you can't be angry, sad, or deeply impacted by it.

What happened to you is not your fault. You did not deserve it. But it is your responsibility to heal. It is not fair, but it is reality.

WORKSHEET 12

Here's one way you can practice accepting your internal experience as it is now. First, identify that there is resistance to accepting the reality of your internal experience. It may sound like this inside:

- This isn't really happening. I don't have parts.

- You're/I'm just crazy.

- How do I know I'm not just making all this up?

- It must be something else—a brain tumor or something.

- You're/I'm an idiot, dumb, stupid for thinking its DID.

We acknowledge that resistance can also present in other ways, such as Headmates pulling you out of front as a way to avoid it, pushing flashbacks forward, or downing the System altogether.

Try writing below what it sounds like in your head when you notice resistance or writing other ways you've noticed resistance come up.

_____

_____

_____

_____

_____

_____

Next, we want to use accepting statements consciously and intentionally after we identify the resistance.

WORKSHEET 13

Some statements that can help with accepting your internal experience may sound like:

- I may not know or understand what is happening inside, but I understand it is for a reason, and that reason is to keep us all safe in some way or to protect us.

- I am part of a System that is designed to keep us all safe and protect us. I am not alone.

- I may not have as much connection to my internal world as I'd like right now, but I understand there is a reason for that, and that reason is to keep me safe or protect me in some way.

- DID is more prevalent than schizophrenia, so it can't be that "crazy" to have DID.

SYSTEM-FRIENDLY TIPS

A note to protectors: Accepting the internal experience does not mean sharing information about the System, trauma memories, and so on.

Now try creating your own statement that can help with accepting your internal experience. These will be called on when we hear our thoughts of resistance.

_____

_____

_____

_____

_____

_____

_____

UNDERSTANDING OUR BEHAVIOR

SOMETIMES, LIFE IS LIKE A MOVIE

Your behaviors can be understood as a series of events. These events are connected to each other, creating a narrative or story. To understand your behaviors, we need to understand the whole story.

Think of it like this: Suddenly, you are watching a movie. It is two-thirds of the way through. The story is at the climax, the big fight scene. Right after the fight scene is over, the movie stops. You are then asked to answer the questions below in detail:

1. Who are all the characters involved in the scene?

2. What was happening before the big fight scene?

3. How do all the characters know each other?

4. Were there characters that weren't in the fight scene that were important to the overall narrative of the movie?

5. Why were they fighting in the first place?

As a System, it can often feel like this. Sometimes you come to front and you're in the middle of what appears to be the end of a fight scene or some intense situation and are expected to be able to answer all the questions above.

It would be very challenging indeed not only to answer those questions but also to understand the answers on a personal level. This is an experience that Systems, unlike singlets, experience as part of their multiplicity.

So let's see if we can develop a formula to help figure out the answers to the questions you may have when you come to front either midway through a fight scene or at the end of a fight scene.

Step 1. Acknowledge that you are fronting and have missed part of the story.

- Validate your experience as a Headmate within the System. Yes, it can be scary to front and not know what is going on. That is why we are developing this formula.

- Denying that you've missed some of the plotline doesn't help you in the long run or move toward the goal of Functional Multiplicity and strong, healthy internal relationships.

Step 2. Describe the environment you are in and what you are noticing now that you are fronting.

- What environment are you in? What room of the house? Sitting down or standing up? Is there anything around you or in your hands?

- Collect as much data as you can. This will help build an idea of what parts of the plotline have been missed.

Step 3. Take a moment and ask inside, What was happening right before I fronted?

- There is never a guarantee that you'll get an answer. Sometimes there is no answer because of a lack of connection with other Headmates. Sometimes there is no answer because there is a communication barrier between you. Sometimes it is deemed unsafe for you to be provided the answer.

SYSTEM-FRIENDLY TIPS

When asking inside about what was happening right before you fronted, be sure to follow up with the reason for asking. This can assist your protectors in determining whether any information is provided at all, or whether some information can be provided. It could sound something like this: "Hey, [Protector Name]. I just fronted and have no idea what is going on. I want to make sure we are safe. Can you tell me anything about what was happening right before I fronted so that I can make sure we are all OK?"

Step 4. Using Logic Mind and your skills of pattern recognition, come up with some options about what may have led to what is happening.

- For example, you have fronted in the kitchen and are holding a knife. You look around and see that there is some food on the counter, half cut. You touch the food itself and notice that it should be cold, but is a bit warm. You conclude that someone was likely cutting up some food and that it has been out for a while as it is no longer cold. You look at the clock and see that it is 6 p.m. and determine that the food being cut is likely for dinner. A Protector has stated "someone was triggered." You conclude that something has occurred during the meal preparation to trigger another Headmate.

Step 5. Identify damage or other unhelpful consequences.

- Here is where you look over the body and ensure that there is no damage, essentially determining whether self-harm has occurred as a result of someone being triggered.

- Remember, the body can experience damage as a result of present-day harm, while you may not experience the sensation of physical pain. It is important for the safety of the System that damage and wounds are tended to appropriately.

First, we do these five steps. Then we can go into how to make changes to our behaviors. We can't change what we don't know or acknowledge.

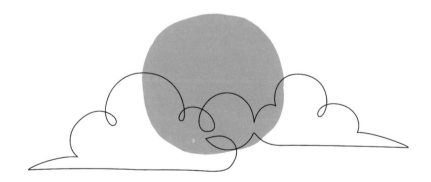

UNDERSTANDING OUR BEHAVIOR

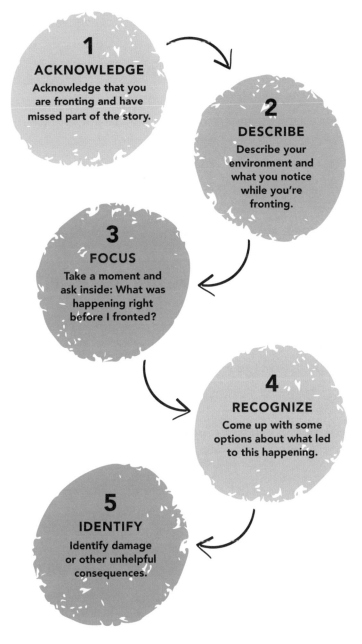

1
ACKNOWLEDGE
Acknowledge that you
are fronting and have
missed part of the story.

2
DESCRIBE
Describe your
environment and
what you notice
while you're
fronting.

3
FOCUS
Take a moment and
ask inside: What was
happening right
before I fronted?

4
RECOGNIZE
Come up with some
options about what led
to this happening.

5
IDENTIFY
Identify damage
or other unhelpful
consequences.

Figure 2.1. The steps in understanding our behavior

WORKSHEET 14

Step 1. Acknowledge that you are fronting and have missed part of the story. What are some helpful statements you can use to validate your experience?

_____

_____

_____

Step 2. Describe the environment you are in and what you are noticing now that you are fronting. What environment are you in? What room of the house? Sitting down or standing up? Is there anything around you or in your hands?

_____

_____

_____

Step 3. Take a moment and ask inside, What was happening right before I fronted? Write down what information you were given to help put the pieces together.

_____

_____

_____

_____

SYSTEM-FRIENDLY TIPS

Remember, you may not get an answer from anyone inside. That is OK. This may be an area of further development for you and your System: building trust with each other. You can use the "Developing Internal Relationships" module to help this area.

If, at this stage in your journey, there is no answer from inside, consider the below areas you could examine:

A. Physical illness, unbalanced eating or sleeping, injury: you have had a cold for several days; you have no energy left but you need to cook and eat; you were cutting up the food and slipped and cut your finger slightly.

B. Use of drugs or alcohol: misuse of prescription drugs, you forgot your medication, alcohol was consumed when it isn't normally, you took a double dose.

C. Stressful events in the environment: a loud noise, a person suddenly entering the room, the food texture was overstimulating.

D. Intense emotions: sadness, anger, fear, loneliness of your own or from another Headmate.

E. Previous behaviors of your own that you found stressful coming into your mind: reminders.

SYSTEM-FRIENDLY TIPS

In the preceding examples, we use the word *you* to refer to anyone internally wanting to engage in this exercise.

Step 4. Using Logic Mind and your skills of pattern recognition, come up with some options about what may have led to what is happening. In the beginning, this may be educated guesses as you develop the skill of recognizing patterns with how your System reacts and responds to things.

_____

_____

_____

Step 5. Identify damage or other unhelpful consequences. It is up to you how you'd like to note down this information. You are welcome to be as candid as you'd like, or simply just add "damage found" and the first aid provided to the body.

_____

_____

_____

Now for the last step in the process. What do I do next?

Step 6. Identify what can be done, right now, as a way to help the System return to a state of calm, to feel validated, and to feel cared for.

- This step is essential in taking a proactive step in moving toward Functional Multiplicity.

- Acknowledging that although you may have only just fronted, and were not part of the events that took place before right now or contributed to the plotline so far, you can indeed change the way the story is going.

This may be something that you decide on your own, using common sense to determine what the next best steps are. However, we encourage you to ask inside again for suggestions or recommendations about what to do next.

Write below what suggestions are offered by the internal team—and what options you yourself have come up with.

_____

_____

_____

_____

_____

_____

_____

_____

_____

SYSTEM-FRIENDLY TIPS

Asking inside about what may be suggested to help move forward in a healthy and validating way may be as simple as stopping whatever activity was being done and distracting with another more pleasant activity. This could be playing your music playlist or going to your couch and cuddling up with your toys. You could phrase your question like this:

"Hey, [Team or Specific Headmates]. I understand someone has been triggered [this validates what has happened]. Is there anything specific you think would help them feel more comfortable, safer, or taken care of?"

Or:

"Hey, [Team or Specific Headmates]. I understand something has happened and now I am fronting. Is there anything specific that I can do to help us feel more comfortable, safer, or taken care of?"

NEED A COLORING BREAK?

Managing Our Emotions Skills

- Understanding My Emotions
- I Know What I Feel—What Now?
- Thinking Purple
- Difficult Emotions Decision Tree

UNDERSTANDING MY EMOTIONS

WHAT ARE THEY?

An emotion can be defined as a complex experience of consciousness that reflects the personal significance of a thing, event, or situation. Emotions will be accompanied by:

- body sensations, often called somatic experiences
- behaviors or behavioral reactions
- thoughts

THE PURPOSE OF EMOTIONS

Our emotions can be described as an expression of our spirit. They can help communicate to us that something is happening deep within that needs to be acknowledged, heard, and actioned. Emotions have a purpose and a function. They are a valuable signal or cue that communicates something to us.

Reminder: You can experience passive influence from a Headmate, where the emotion can feel "mine but not mine." This is one way Headmates can communicate with you.

SYSTEM-FRIENDLY TIPS

Each Headmate may only experience a few emotions, or none at all if they are dissociated from emotions. You can use this section to better understand emotions as individual Headmates and as a System.

THE EMOTION WHEEL

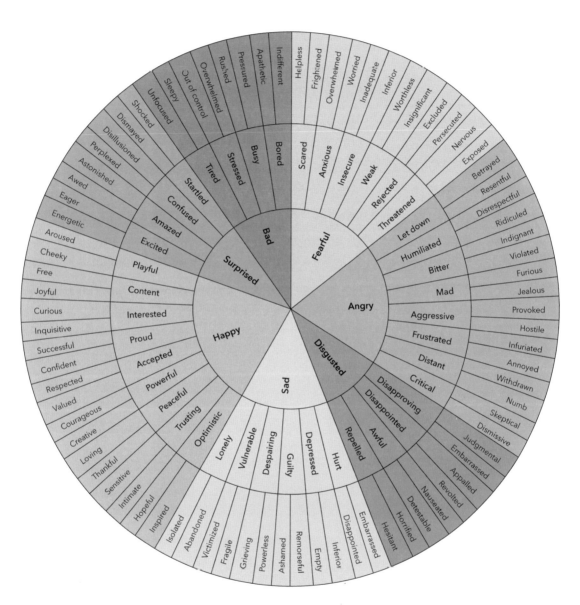

Figure 3.1.

ALEXITHYMIA

Alexithymia is when you have difficulty experiencing, identifying, and expressing emotions. This is different from the emotional dissociation you can experience as a System.

Think of emotional dissociation as a transient (lasting a short time) experience and a disconnection with the experience of emotions. Alexithymia, or emotional blindness, is something that occurs on an ongoing basis and reflects a cognitive state of externally oriented thinking with an inability to identify and label basic and core emotions, like those at the center of the Emotion Wheel—for example, identifying disgust and anger as different and separate emotional experiences.

In working on understanding your emotions, it can be helpful to better understand how your brain works. Do you also experience alexithymia? There are a few online tests you can take that are free and can give you an indication about whether alexithymia is something for you to consider:

https://embrace-autism.com

www.alexithymia.us

SYSTEM-FRIENDLY TIPS

Lots of Systems may also have autism, ADHD, or both (AuDHD). It can be helpful to understand whether your experiences with emotions are part of being an allistic or neurotypical System or a neurodivergent System. It is common for folks who have complex post-traumatic stress disorder (CPTSD) to also experience alexithymia. You are encouraged to talk more about alexithymia with your treating therapist.

THE PURPOSE OF EMOTIONS

This is a simplified way of looking at the function of our core emotions and what they may be communicating to us. Of course, it is not rigid or exhaustive. I encourage you to discuss with your treater about your own emotional experiences to get a deeper understanding.

Note that these relate to emotions, not trauma responses.

ANGRY

A violation of an expectation has occurred. You expected something to happen or not happen, or you expected another to do or not do something. For example, the other person did not follow through with something that I believed we both understood as being agreed to between us (the System) and you (the other person).

FEARFUL

Fear can be experienced when we are uncertain of the outcome of an event or interaction. More specifically, our mind asks, What if …? Typically, your mind will fill in the blanks or answer the "what if" question. Fear can be experienced as an alert to a *perceived known* negative outcome where our mind assumes probability rather than possibility.

Perceived known: something that we think we know. It does not necessarily mean we are correct or not. It simply describes our belief that we know the outcome.

SURPRISED

Something unexpected has occurred or not occurred. You are experiencing, suddenly, a new stimulus or piece of information. For example, a loud sound has unexpectedly occurred, and I was unprepared for it.

BAD

We can feel bad when we are understimulated or overstimulated. Is there too much or not enough sensory input? Consider all your senses: auditory, visual, touch and texture, smell, taste, proprioception (your sense of where your body is in relation to objects and in open spaces), and interoception (what we are feeling on the inside—pain, thirst, the urge to use the bathroom, and other sensations or emotions).

DISGUSTED

The feeling of disgust can be quite uncomfortable. However, it too is telling us something. It can be a response of rejection of something, typically something that is not in line with our values. It is an intense dislike of something. It is related to shame, but a different emotion.

SAD

Sadness can occur when we feel we have lost something. When we feel we have lost a connection with someone, when we feel a loss of control, our independence, or choice. We can also feel sad when we feel a loss of our sense of belonging or something we thought we had or could have in the future.

HAPPY

Experiencing happiness can be difficult, especially if you have survived significant trauma. It is important to acknowledge this for some Headmates as both normal and valid. We generally experience being happy when we are living a life in line with our values.

ASHAMED

Unlike disgust, which is a rejection of some*thing*, shame is a strong negative emotion characterized by the rejection of self. A person who experiences shame perceives themselves as less than. It typically sounds like "I am" statements: I am bad; I am unworthy; I am nothing.

I KNOW WHAT I FEEL—WHAT NOW?

Note that this module on emotions does not relate to trauma responses or flashbacks.

1. **Validate.** This is always the first step when it comes to emotions. No ifs, buts, or maybes. Validating your emotions should be the very first thing you do. Use the worksheet in this module to see how to practice validating your emotions.

2. **Check the Facts.** Now you know what you are feeling, and generally why you may be feeling this way, and you've validated that it is OK to have this feeling. Next, we check whether the intensity of this feeling matches the current reality—the present moment—or if we may be bringing in past events and unresolved emotions from these events. This can happen often for Systems as there are often many unresolved and unhealed events. Your emotions are still valid, even when the intensity of the feelings is informed by the past.

3. **Time to Think Purple.** Thinking Purple is our way of describing Wise Mind used within the original DBT framework. Thinking Purple is about integrating logic and emotion together to create a wise approach to things. With Thinking Purple, we are integrating those more emotionally driven Headmates, denoted by the color red, and your more logic-driven Headmates, denoted by the color blue. Mixed together, creating a wise path forward, we have our beautiful purple.

SYSTEM-FRIENDLY TIPS

Validating the emotions of all Headmates can be difficult at times, depending on who they are, for example Introjects, or how intense the emotion being experienced is, as for Headmates with extreme experiences of shame. Remember, you get to choose which exercises you are ready to do and which ones you want to skip for now.

WORKSHEET 15

Validation is always your first step when it comes to emotions—*every single time.* But what does this look like, exactly? Validating your emotions or those of your Headmates means that you not only see and hear the emotions but also accept the existence of the emotions.

Let's consider the opposite: what invalidating emotions might look like. To invalidate an emotion means to ignore it, pretend it isn't happening, acknowledge it is happening but reject it, or judge it as wrong or not allowed.

Having a list of statements you can read may help in the beginning when practicing validating your emotions. Take a moment and think about what they may sound like. Write some down below.

_____

_____

_____

_____

_____

_____

_____

_____

_____

_____

WORKSHEET 16

Here are some examples you could use to start off. These can be said out loud or inside the Headspace. They can be directed inward, where you are setting the intention for your Headmates to hear these statements:

- I hear you. Your emotions are not too much. I am not going anywhere.

- You are allowed to feel [emotion word]. You have a lot to feel [emotion word] about.

- [If we don't know the specific emotion:] I know you are overwhelmed right now. Your feelings are not too much.

You can even add some additional information about the purpose of emotions to help validate those emotions experienced. For example:

- I hear you. You are angry. Your anger helps us or helps me understand that something isn't quite right.

- I see, feel, or hear how sad you are, [Headmate's name]. You have so much to be sad about. We have lost so much. It is OK to be sad. You are not alone. I am here with you.

CHECK THE FACTS

When we are experiencing intense feelings, our brains will use old patterns or formulas to answer the question, Why is this situation happening?

Our brain wants to interpret the situation and create meaning from the situation. Essentially, what do the situation and the intense feelings mean about how we belong in the world, about the relationship we are in, or about ourselves as a person?

The brain will use these patterns or formulas that were developed early on in life regardless of whether they apply in the present moment or not—unless we slow things down and question them.

SYSTEM-FRIENDLY TIPS

Validating can be challenging when we don't know what we may be feeling, especially if there are several Headmates that are experiencing feelings all at once. Go back to the Emotion Wheel (figure 3.1) and take some time to see what words jump out at you and how you all may be feeling. Remember, take your time here. If you are feeling overwhelmed, you don't have to do this exercise right away. You get to choose when you do these exercises.

Here's an example. Maybe you were expecting to video chat with a System friend on Wednesday, but they never called. You feel disappointed, sad, rejected, and lonely.

You may have the thought, *My friend never talks to us,* which may lead to the thought, *My friend doesn't even care about us,* and then the thought, *No one cares about us,* and then, *We are going to be alone forever,* and so on. These thoughts may seem reasonable at the time as it may certainly feel this way.

But feelings are not facts. All feelings are valid, and all feelings communicate something to us about how a situation has impacted us. The facts, however, are the things that actually happened in the situation. The facts could be:

- what was said: the words used
- when things occurred: the date, the year, and so on
- who was there and who was not there
- the intention behind what was said

Understanding what someone's intention is when something is said or done is not something we should typically assume. You cannot read another person's mind.

You can interpret based on a pattern of behavior seen in others, or the pattern of behavior seen with that person specifically. However, this is never a guarantee that this equals and is objectively their intention. More on others' intentions appears in "People and Parts Relationship Skills," later in the workbook.

Checking the facts is an important step to use when you are experiencing intense feelings and want to feel calmer, more grounded, and in the now. The following worksheets can help develop the skill to check the facts.

WORKSHEET 17

Ask yourself the five questions below. An example of how this worksheet could be filled out is on the following pages.

1. What emotion is particularly difficult, hardest to sit with, or currently stuck on repeat?

_____

_____

_____

_____

_____

_____

2. What is the prompting event of the intense feeling above? Describe the situation itself and what happened right before the intense emotion came up.

_____

_____

_____

_____

_____

3. What are your interpretations, thoughts, and the meaning you've assigned about the event? This can also include your interpretation of the other person's intentions.

_____

_____

_____

_____

4. With the current feelings out of the mix, what are other possible interpretations of the event? Use pure Logic Mind.

_____

_____

_____

_____

5. Am I assuming a threat exists? Label the threat. Identify it exactly. For example, "We are going to be alone forever" is threatening because of the "being alone forever" part.

_____

_____

_____

WORKSHEET 17 EXAMPLE

1. What emotion is particularly difficult, hardest to sit with, or currently stuck on repeat?

Rejected. I hate this feeling. It is so hard to have. I also feel some shame and anger.

2. What is the prompting event of the intense feeling above? Describe the situation itself and what happened right before the intense emotion came up.

I looked at my phone and noticed it was 4:30 p.m. on Wednesday. I realized my friend hadn't called me. They always call at 4 p.m.

3. What are your interpretations, thoughts, and the meaning you've assigned about the event? This can also include your interpretation of the person's intentions.

I thought they must've finally gotten too tired of hearing about us. I thought that they never call us, not really. I interpreted that, by them not calling, they don't want to be friends anymore. I assigned the meaning that no one would want to be our friend and we will be alone forever and that we are "too much." I assume that they knew how much it would hurt me and still did it—they intended to hurt me.

4. With the current feelings out of the mix, what are other possible interpretations of the event?

Maybe something happened and they can't get to the phone right now.

Maybe their phone died.

Maybe they forgot what day it was.

Maybe they lost track of time and didn't realize they missed our call.

Maybe they aren't doing well themselves and couldn't do a phone call.

Maybe they forgot about the call (innocently) but didn't know how to say sorry and was worried I would hate them.

5. Am I assuming a threat exists? Label the threat. Identify it exactly.

Yes. I am assuming that a threat exists.

I assume we will be alone forever and that no one will want to be our friend. I am also assuming that they intentionally did this to me, that they knew it would hurt me and did it anyway. The threat is that I can't trust them now because they wanted to hurt me.

SYSTEM-FRIENDLY TIPS

The fourth question helps us later on when using Thinking Purple, our version of Wise Mind. It helps us bring some logic into the mix. Remember, as a System you are working toward Functional Multiplicity. Part of that is working as a team. Try inviting those Headmates whose strength is working in logic without emotionality.

Now that we have validated our feelings and we have checked the facts, we understand more about the situation and how our feelings have been influenced by our thinking patterns. Perhaps we have identified that we were out of our Window of Tolerance as well:

We feel rejected, sad, and lonely. That is OK, we are allowed to have these feelings. There is no wrong way to feel.

Some of us felt immediately really angry and wanted to text them right away how hurtful they are.

I hate feeling rejected. The feeling came up when I saw the time on my phone. It was thirty minutes past our agreed time. It led to me feeling threatened that we would be alone forever. And that this friend hates us. I noticed that our body went tense and the heart rate went really fast. I noticed some of us were in flight more and others may have been in fight mode.

Next, we put it all together and use the Thinking Purple process. Integrating both the hot, intense emotional experience (red) with the logical and rationale mind (blue). Together they create a wise purple mind.

THINKING **PURPLE**

This is the System-friendly adaptation to Wise Mind. In DBT, Wise Mind is described as the meeting or synthesis of the Emotion Mind and the Logic Mind. The System-friendly version considers the Logic Mind as those Headmates with a more rational or logical focus. It also considers the Emotion Mind as those Headmates who experience intense and strong emotions and who may often feel consumed by their emotions.

LOGIC MIND

Headmates who tend to:

- Be cold and shut off from emotions
- Be ruled by facts and logic
- Be task-focused
- Be able to ignore emotions or think they are useless
- Feel more mechanical

EMOTION MIND

Headmates who tend to:

- Be ruled by their moods, feelings, and impulses
- Not consider logic and only consider emotions
- Be impulsive and act on their feelings quickly

THINKING **PURPLE**

In order to Think Purple, we first must acknowledge the value and importance of all Headmates.

Thinking Purple works on integrating the wisdom of both logic and emotion and seeing the value in both—adding the red with the blue to create purple. We understand that although the intensity of our emotions may not match the event itself or fit the facts of the event, our emotions are always valid and are communicating something.

SYSTEM-FRIENDLY TIPS

Integration, unlike Fusion, is the building of relationships between Headmates. Fusion is when two or more Headmates coalesce (come together) to form a new Headmate, a combination of all that were involved in the process. In this context, we are using the word *integration* to describe the coming together of two colors, our red and blue—essentially describing the collaboration of our two Headmates to develop a purple or wise path forward.

WORKSHEET 18

LOGIC MIND

Who are my Headmates who tend to be logic-driven?

_____

_____

_____

_____

_____

_____

EMOTION MIND

Who are my Headmates who tend to be emotion-driven?

_____

_____

_____

_____

_____

_____

THINKING **PURPLE**

How to Think Purple. Fill in the blanks:

I am feeling (label the emotions; you can use the Emotion Wheel, figure 3.1, to help).

_____

_____

_____

And I feel this way because (refresh your memory on the purpose of emotions and apply your unique experience to the emotions named above).

_____

_____

_____

_____

And (this is where we add logic into the mix).

_____

_____

_____

_____

Let's look at an example.

WORKSHEET 18 EXAMPLE

LOGIC MIND

Who are my Headmates who tend to be logic-driven?

• *Terri*

He is often described as cold and unfeeling but really helps me make decisions.

EMOTION MIND

Who are my Headmates who tend to be emotion-driven?

• *Noom*

They struggle when I feel sad. It feels like I fall into a dark hole and there is no way out.

*THINKING **PURPLE***

How to Think Purple. Fill in the blanks:

I am feeling (label the emotions; you can use the Emotion Wheel, figure 3.1, to help).

I feel rejected, sad, and lonely.

And I feel this way because (refresh your memory on the purpose of emotions and apply your unique experience to the emotions named above).

A friend didn't call me when we agreed to call at 4 p.m. It is now 4:30 p.m. I feel sad because I feel like I may have lost a friend. I feel rejected by this friend. I feel lonely because I normally have someone to talk to at this time; that has been our routine. It is OK to feel this way; I am allowed to have feelings; These emotions are valid.

And (this is where we add logic into the mix).

And I understand that maybe my friend may have lost track of time or had another reasonable explanation that meant that we weren't all on the call.

DIFFICULT EMOTIONS DECISION TREE

Having a strong emotion and a hard time deciding what to do next? That's OK. Remember, when we are out of our Window of Tolerance, decision-making can be really hard.

Using what you've learned so far in this module, write down the identifiable emotions on the Difficult Emotions Decision Tree. Move through the tree and arrive at the most effective next steps.

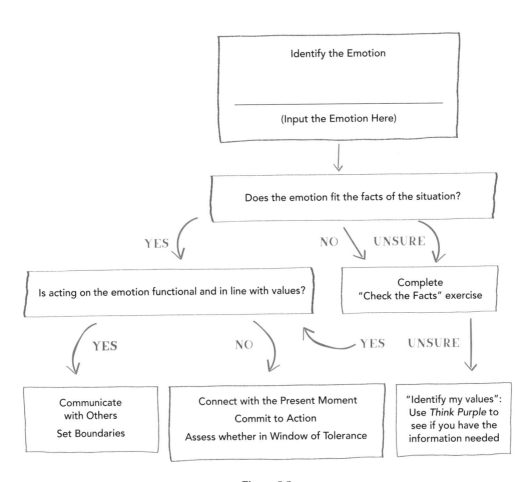

Figure 3.2.

NEED A COLORING BREAK?

Values-Guided Action Skills

- Identifying Our Values
- Committing to Action
- Steering Our Ship

IDENTIFYING OUR VALUES

Knowing what your values are can be helpful in creating System rules or guidelines. As a System, it is important that all Headmates are aware of these values so that when fronting they can make choices that are in line with these values. Consider this your Systems code or creed to live by.

WHAT ARE VALUES?

Values are a person's beliefs about what's important, or what matters most to them. They can be just about anything, such as honesty, respect, success, or peace. Sometimes people lose sight of their values—they live their life in a way that doesn't match or is out of alignment with what they believe. For example, someone who values authenticity may become overwhelmed at work when talking in the break room about a TV show they like, when everyone else is saying they don't like it.

Values can be thought of as a direction, like north, west, and so on. Values are not something we achieve—we can't "achieve" north. We can travel in the direction of north and make decisions to continue to head in that direction.

For yourselves, consider this exercise to determine your Systems values. You could think of it as your System Creed. A creed means a set of beliefs or aims that guide your actions.

Look at the values list and complete the following exercise to get a clearer idea of your Systems values. And yes, there are a lot of them.

acceptance	accomplishment	accountability	accuracy	achievement
adaptability	alertness	altruism	ambition	amusement
assertiveness	attentiveness	authenticity	awareness	balance
beauty	boldness	bravery	brilliance	calm
candor	capableness	carefulness	certainty	challenge
charity	cleanliness	clearness	cleverness	comfort
commitment	communication	community	compassion	competence
concentration	confidence	connection	consciousness	consistency
contentment	contribution	control	conviction	cooperation
courage	courtesy	creation	creativity	credibility
curiosity	decisiveness	dedication	dependability	determination
development	dignity	discipline	discovery	drive
effectiveness	efficiency	empathy	empowerment	endurance
energy	enjoyment	enthusiasm	equality	ethicalness
excellence	experience	exploration	expressiveness	fairness
motivation	openness	optimism	order	organization
originality	passion	patience	peace	performance
persistence	playfulness	poise	potential	power
presentness	productivity	professionalism	prosperity	purpose
quality	realism	reason	recognition	recreation
reflectiveness	respect	responsibility	restraint	results
reverence	rigor	risk	satisfaction	security
selflessness	self-reliance	sense	sensitivity	serenity
service	sharing	significance	simplicity	sincerity
skillfulness	smartness	solitude	spirit	spirituality
spontaneousness	stability	status	stewardship	strength
structure	success	support	surprise	sustainability
talent	teamwork	temperance	thankfulness	thoroughness
thoughtfulness	timeliness	tolerance	toughness	traditionality
tranquility	transparency	trustingness	trustworthiness	truth
understanding	uniqueness	unity	valor	victory
vigor	vision	vitality	wealth	welcoming
winning	wisdom	wonder	work	

WORKSHEET 19

Instructions:

1. Read through the values list and get a feel for what is on it. There's no need to do anything yet.

2. Sit for a moment and let the list sink in to those Headmates who are engaging with the exercise.

3. Read over the list again. Using a pen or a highlighter, mark the top ten that stand out to you, in no particular order. Trust that they will jump out at you. List your top ten:

1.

_____

2.

_____

3.

_____

4.

_____

5.

_____

6.

_____

7.

_____

8.

_____

9.

_____

10.

_____

4. Now go through those top ten and select your top five, again in no particular order. List them below:

1.

_____

2.

_____

3.

_____

4.

_____

5.

_____

5. Now, using your top five list, spend some time defining these values. What do they mean to you? What does it look like when you are making choices in line with each value? For example:

Respect. I define this as accepting somebody for who they are, even when they're different from me or I don't agree with them.

_____

_____

_____

_____

_____

_____

_____

_____

_____

_____

_____

_____

_____

_____

COMMITTING TO ACTION

Now that you are more familiar with your values, your System Creed, you can start to become more comfortable with how your System will likely respond or behave in specific situations. Essentially, this is designed to help you feel comfortable when you are not fronting or when you're back in the Headspace, so that the decisions being made are in line with the System Creed or values.

QUESTIONS TO ASK

When making a decision about how to respond to a situation, person, event, and so on, you can ask yourself, or the System in general, these questions:

1. What is important to me or to us in this situation? For example, is it important for me or for us to be honest, spontaneous, reliable?

2. What is the outcome I would like from this situation? For example, a resolution, to be right, justice, etc.

It may sound like this:

1. *It is important to us that we are reliable when it comes to friends. However, it is also important to us to be honest with ourselves and take care of our mental health.*

2. *The outcome we'd like to see is that our friend understands that we are reliable and care about them and the friendship, but our mental health comes first and sometimes we may need to cancel or reschedule plans.*

AN EXAMPLE SITUATION

Not in line with your values:

Say nothing, ignoring your friends' messages when they ask if you are online on Wednesday night. Avoid the topic till the week later. Say nothing to them the next week and keep changing the topic when asked about it.

In line with your values:

Message your friend, saying, "I don't have capacity to chat tonight. I appreciate your friendship but need a couple days to recuperate. I will text you in a few days to check in."

Using the example above, what values do you think this person may hold and use to influence their decision? There are no wrong answers.

_____

_____

_____

_____

_____

_____

_____

SYSTEM-FRIENDLY TIPS

With a number of Headmates, everyone's values are important and valid. As such, making a decision that reflects the whole System can be difficult as you develop your internal relationships and better System communication. Be patient with yourselves—you are all learning to manage and share one life, together.

STEERING OUR SHIP

You have learned how to identify your values as an individual and as a System, and you can now more comfortably make a decision in the moment that displays real commitment to these values. Now let's talk about steering our ship in the overall direction we want our life to go.

When we talk about steering our ship, we go back to thinking of our values as a direction, like north or west. The ship itself is the body, the vessel that contains your consciousness. The crewmates of your ship are your entire System. Some of the decks we know about, and some we aren't yet aware of. Some Headmates, or crewmates, we know of, and some we aren't yet aware of. You are all on this ship sailing the seas of life.

As the members of the ship, you are all steering in the direction of your values, the System Creed. Each moment in life is an opportunity to head in that direction. But life isn't always calm waters. Life can throw anything at us at any time. Sometimes it can be a strong gust of wind that knocks us off course; sometimes we may spring a leak. Sometimes we get nice weather, sailing along smoothly, and sometimes there is a major storm that feels like it will never end and we are going to capsize. This is all a normal part of being alive—and yes, at times it can suck.

When we get knocked off course, we could scream and yell, blame ourselves, totally give up, or impulsively do something to try to make things feel better in that moment. But how much would that actually help in the long run? Instead, we could slow down and assess the damage. For example:

- How far off course are we from where we'd like to be?

- What contributed to us being off course?

- What could we do to correct course?

Try this next exercise when you feel off course.

WORKSHEET 20

Define the situation. What happened to get us off course?

_____

_____

_____

_____

_____

_____

Which values can we identify that have been impacted? For example, we've been keeping secrets from a good friend, but we really value honesty. Go back to "Identifying Our Values" earlier in this section to remind you of your values.

_____

_____

_____

_____

_____

_____

What nonjudgmental statements can we make to ourselves? This is designed to help you increase self-compassion. This is where we can use our Thinking Purple statements.

_____

_____

_____

_____

_____

Now identify what you are going to do—what committed actions you are going to take to correct your course?

For example, this may include letting your friend know that you've been afraid to tell them something. If you are not sure how to communicate this, don't worry. That's in the next module, "People and Parts Relationship Skills."

_____

_____

_____

_____

_____

_____

People and Parts Relationship Skills

- Communicating with Others
- Considering Intention and Impact
- Setting Boundaries
- Developing Internal Relationships

COMMUNICATING WITH OTHERS

WHY IT'S IMPORTANT

When building healthy interpersonal relationships—relationships with external folks—it is important to understand that open, clear, and honest communication is foundational. Communication is sending or receiving information. It sounds simple enough, but in reality, there are so many things that can go wrong. Some myths about communication and interpersonal relationships:

- If I say it a certain way or the right way, they won't get upset.

- If they say no, it means they hate me or the relationship is over.

- I don't deserve to get what I want or need.

- If I make a request or ask for what I need, this will show that I am a weak or vulnerable person.

- I have to know whether a person is going to say yes before I make a request.

- If I make a request or ask for what I need, I am being selfish or burdening the other person.

- If someone doesn't do something I've asked, it means they don't care about me.

SYSTEM-FRIENDLY TIPS

With several Headmates, the way in which you can communicate with others can be varied: verbal, written, in person, voice memo, sign language, visual cues through drawings, music, and more.

THE POWER OF LANGUAGE

The words we choose when communicating with others are important. Each word chosen has a specific meaning we have constructed from our own experiences. The word *nice* can mean different things depending on the meaning we assign to that word. As such, it is important that when communicating with others, we do so with intention.

First, we need to consider what the intended message is, asking yourself, the sender, what it is we want this other person to know. If you aren't sure where to begin, you can use the statements below to help begin identifying what your intended message may be.

- *I don't like something that you have done.*

- *I don't like something that you have not done.* Or: *I expected you to do something, but you didn't.*

- *I am afraid of an experience that I am anticipating may happen.*

- *I have been triggered by something you have done or not done.*

SYSTEM-FRIENDLY TIPS

Triggers remind you of traumatic events or negative experiences. The reaction of being triggered could be in the form of painful memories, emotional distress, a panic attack, or flashbacks. Being triggered is not the same thing as feeling uncomfortable, or the feelings you get if you disagree with something.

WORKSHEET 21

1. Use the space below to write what you are trying to communicate. This is your first draft, so write what first comes to mind. Use this first draft to express your feelings and thoughts without judgment or overthinking it. This will then be used to help refine your message.

   Ask yourselves: **What would we really want to say if we had the opportunity to say whatever we want, however we want, totally unedited?**

   _____

   _____

   _____

We can now use the above to identify the key points of our intended message. Below is an example of what you could write. Background: You and a friend had a phone call where your singlet friend said:

   I totally understand. Sometimes I feel like I am different people too.

SYSTEM-FRIENDLY TIPS

Use the "Managing Our Emotions Skills" module to help identify how you may be feeling.

Ask yourselves: **What would we really want to say if we had the opportunity to say whatever we want, however we want, totally unedited?**

When you [the friend] said that you totally understood because sometimes you feel like you're different people, it really hurt. We felt so invalidated. Some of my Headmates feel like we can't trust you anymore, and that makes us sad. It feels like you don't even understand us and how hard it is to be a System and that you think it's just this fun thing where you get to be different people whenever you want. But it's really fucking hard, every day, and what you said hurt. And I need you to apologize and understand how you made us feel, and some of us will need to build trust again.

2. Now that we have the "warts and all" version of our message, we can refine it into the key points. We do this by identifying the feelings experienced. Use the "Managing Our Emotions Skills" module to help.

    Using the example above, the emotions experienced are:

    • hurt

    • feeling invalidated

    • sadness

    • fear that we can't trust our friend

    • anger

Write below what emotions you experienced when looking over your first draft. Remember, all feelings are valid.

_____

_____

_____

3. We now have your first draft, the initial reaction to what has happened. We also have refined that draft to identify the emotions we experienced as part of our response. Let's start putting together a script to communicate this to the other person. In line with DBT skills, let's use the acronym DEAR MAN:

D—DESCRIBE

Describe the situation. Stick to the facts. Tell the person exactly what you are reacting to—the event that has led to the emotional experiences that you identified earlier. Try to be concise.

Avoid using the words *always* and *never.* Typically, it is inaccurate to say it is literally 100 percent of the time.

SYSTEM-FRIENDLY TIPS

Try using these details to help create your "Describe."

When

- the date, if it has been a little while; e.g. "last month"
- the day, if more recently; e.g. "on Monday"
- the event, e.g. "X's party"

What

- the words the person used, if it was a specific word
- the behavior, if the person acted a certain way

E—EXPRESS

Express your feelings about the situation. Don't assume that the other person knows how you feel. People can't read our minds, even though that would be nice. It may seem very obvious to you, but don't assume it is obvious to them.

SYSTEM-FRIENDLY TIPS

Use "I" statements and avoid starting a sentence with "you."

When we start a sentence with "you," it can be interpreted as critical or attacking. Remember when communicating with others that we want them to hear our intended message. When others feel criticized or attacked, they will likely become defensive and not hear what you have to say. Of course, if you are out with the person you are communicating with, the "I" statement will be a "we" statement.

A—ASSERT

Assert yourself by asking for what you want or need. Generally, our focus here is what you want, not what you don't want. For example, *"I would like you to ask more questions about my experiences."*

An exception can be when you are setting a specific boundary, like *"I do not want to be touched"* or *"I do not want to continue this relationship."*

SYSTEM-FRIENDLY TIPS

These conversations can be really hard to have with someone. If you are worried about forgetting what you want to say, or getting off track, or having a Headmate switch in that may not have the right words, try writing this down as a literal script. This can help stay on track and help other Headmates know what the System wants to say collectively. You can always add, "This conversation is really important to us, so we wrote down what we wanted to say."

R—REINFORCE

Reinforce to the person the positive effects of you getting what you are asking for. For example, *"When you ask questions about my experiences, it shows me you care."*

If you think it is helpful, you can clarify the negative consequences of not getting what you want or need, like, *"When you don't ask me questions, it feels like you're making assumptions."*

Don't forget to reinforce the desired behavior after the fact. This can help the other person remember that this is a behavior we want or need. It can sound like *"I really appreciate when you asked me what my experiences of X were."*

M—MESSAGE (IN DBT: MINDFUL)

Keep your focus on your goal of the communication, what the message you want to deliver is. It can be hard when having the conversation and you feel anxious; that's why writing it down can help. Saying that you've written it down can also show to the other person how important this conversation is to you. We want to stay on track with the message and not get off-topic and distracted.

Again, avoid using the words *always* and *never,* as this can lead you down a rabbit hole.

Essentially, you are a broken record when it comes to your message. Keep asking, saying no, or expressing your opinion over and over. We might need to do this if the other person starts to use *always* and *never* language.

If the other person feels criticized or attacked, they can be defensive. Sometimes the best defense is an offense: to attack or criticize back. Where you can, do not engage in their content, as it can get you off track with your message. Let's call this reactivity. When trying to communicate with others, sometimes they can become reactive—they feel attacked, shut down, and become defensive, or go on the offense. If this happens, it may be time to set a boundary. Not sure how? That's our next module.

A—APPEAR CONFIDENT

Appear confident in what you are saying. Notice we are saying "appear" confident—we don't expect you to magically become confident in these conversations. Sometimes you have to fake it till you make it. Like with any skill, practicing improves your capability.

N—NEGOTIATE

This does not mean to fawn, people-please, or give up your stance. The purpose of negotiation is to arrange or settle by discussion and mutual agreement. This can include asking the other person what they think may help in creating a solution.

With our example, it could look like, *"What do you think would help you be more curious?"* This could lead to the person asking for something from you: *"Maybe I could do some more research on this. Do you have any recommendations for sources?"*

Again, this is not where you give up your wants or needs. That would be a fawn response, one of the trauma responses.

SYSTEM-FRIENDLY TIPS

Reflect with your Headmates and identify who may be the most effective at presenting as confident for these conversations. Work together. There is no rule that you can't be co-con (co-conscious) and have a team approaching these conversations, meaning you have a support system in the background who can switch in or simply cheer you on and remind you of the purpose of the conversation.

WORKSHEET 21 EXAMPLE

Reminder: You and a singlet friend were talking on the phone about how difficult it can be to have different Headmates want different things all the time. During the call, your friend said, *"I totally understand. I sometimes feel like I am different people too."*

D—DESCRIBE

When we were on the phone on Wednesday, talking about how hard it is for us, I heard you say that you understood because you sometimes feel like you are different people too.

E—EXPRESS

When we heard that statement, we felt invalidated and hurt, and some of us have been scared to open up again.

A—ASSERT

We would like you to say things like "That makes sense" or "I hear what you're saying" when you are trying to show us understanding.

R—REINFORCE

Statements like that help us feel heard and accepted. The statement before sounds like our experiences are minimized or not important.

M—MESSAGE

What we are trying to say is that the statement hurt our feelings. Our friendship means a lot to us, and we wanted to communicate that and other ways you can show us understanding.

A—APPEAR CONFIDENT

Avoid using words like *just* or *maybe,* as these may appear unconfident. We also want to avoid giving the other person the impression that the emotions expressed and the impact of the situation are not important, or smaller than they actually are.

For example: *"When we heard that statement, it just hurt our feelings. Maybe you could perhaps try something else next time—if that's OK with you."*

N—NEGOTIATE

As in the "A—ASSERT" on the previous page, offering options can help the other person be clearer on what we do want. For example, you could say, "That makes sense" or "I hear what you're saying." As you negotiate with your friend, you could ask them, after providing those two options, if they have any other options they think may work. Here's how it may sound in full:

When we were on the phone on Wednesday, talking about how hard it is for us, I heard you say that you understood because you sometimes feel like you are different people too. When we heard that statement, we felt invalidated and hurt, and some of us have been scared to open up again. We prefer hearing things like "That makes sense" or "I hear what you're saying" when you are trying to show us you understand our experiences. Statements like that help us feel heard and accepted. We feel statements like the one said over the phone sound like our experiences are minimized or not important. What we are trying to say is that the statement hurt our feelings. Our friendship means a lot to us, and we wanted to communicate that and other ways you can show us understanding. Do you have any other ideas for statements like "That makes sense" that you feel work better for you?

WORKSHEET 22

Now you try. Fill out the section below with what your version of DEAR MAN would be using the example in Worksheet 23, or use an example from your own life.

D

_____

E

_____

A

_____

R

_____

M

_____

A

_____

N

_____

CONSIDERING INTENTION AND IMPACT

When building healthy, strong relationships with others, internal and external, it is important to consider two factors: the intention of others who aren't our Headmates, and the impact their behavior has had on you and your system.

INTENTION

Intention is the other person's motives or reason for why they have done something or not done something. It is important that we recognize that people don't just do things—their decisions aren't typically impulsive. When we talk about intention in the context of relationships, we are often referring to a complex mix of conscious and subconscious needs that motivate us to act in certain ways.

CONSCIOUS AND SUBCONSCIOUS INTENTIONS

Conscious intentions are the ones a person is aware of. When asked about it, they can identify, articulate, and explain their reasoning for why they did it or didn't do it. A person's subconscious intentions are those motivations that are below the surface of their awareness. Subconscious intentions are fueled by deeper core beliefs, past experiences, and emotional needs. The person is not aware of how these beliefs, experiences, and needs impact their behavior.

For the most part, people are able to recognize their conscious intentions easily through a process of self-reflection, the process of looking inward and recognizing their patterns of behavior, emotional responses, and the outcomes of their actions in various situations—essentially the "what" of their behavior. True self-awareness, however, requires a person to go beyond self-reflection and take an additional step: introspection. Introspection helps a person uncover their subconscious intentions—the "why" of their behavior.

Understanding the difference between these two types of intention and what is required to identify them is important when it comes to relationships. In relationships with people, there is always conflict. We don't mean fighting, abuse, and screaming matches. Conflict occurs when people have different views, needs, or desires and wants that clash. As part of learning to build and sustain healthy relationships, we need to understand that conflict is inevitable. But what about impact?

IMPACT

Impact is the effects or consequences of the other person's actions on you and your System, regardless of their intentions. Impact is the outcome you experience because of their actions. The outcome can be pleasant, unpleasant, or neutral.

It is important to understand that the relationship between these two concepts—intention and impact—is related but not causational. A person can have every intention of being pleasant, helpful, nice, and loving, and the impact of their behavior can still have an unpleasant impact on you.

A person's intentions do not invalidate the impact their behavior has had on you. This can be a new and confrontational way of looking at things. I often hear, *"But they didn't mean to hurt me."* While this may be true, it does not mean that the impact, the hurt, is invalid or now voided.

The intensity of the impact you experience because of a person's behavior can be influenced by your own core beliefs and past experiences. That's why the "Check the Facts" strategy in "Managing Our Emotions Skills" is important. It can help you understand whether the intensity of the hurt you feel is because of the person's behavior in the now, or whether there are feelings from the past that are also being activated or reexperienced (triggered).

SYSTEM-FRIENDLY TIPS

When we talk about impact as a result of others' intentions, we are not referring to the intentions of those who hurt you all that time ago. For the purposes of this workbook, we are focusing on present-day relationships with the aim to assist you in building your connections with people in the here and now.

WORKSHEET 23

Let's apply our new understanding to an example of a relationship with an external person. You can also use this worksheet to reflect on your internal relationships.

George (System) was talking with Baz (singlet), his friend of three years.

George was discussing how hard it is for them to tell their other friend Carrie (singlet), a friend of one year, that she can sometimes make ableist comments. George told Baz that they understand Carrie doesn't mean to [doesn't intend to] be ableist but that it still hurts when they hear these statements, and they wish that Carrie would put more effort into learning about DID.

After that conversation, Baz decides to talk with Carrie about how hurtful her comments are to George, and that she is ableist and should learn more about DID. Baz then text-messages George, letting him know that he has told Carrie how hurtful she has been to him. George feels betrayed and that Baz is now an unsafe person to be around. To protect himself, George decides to block Baz on all social media and stops returning his text messages.

Reading the above example, what do you think Baz's intentions are?

_____

_____

_____

Now think more deeply about Baz's intentions. What could his conscious intentions be, and what might his subconscious intentions be?

For example, Baz may say he intended to help George [his conscious intentions], but after thinking more deeply about it, Baz acknowledged that he has had past experiences with other uneducated, hurtful statements made about him [subconscious intentions] and wanted to make sure that Carrie wasn't going to be like those other people.

_____

_____

_____

_____

_____

SYSTEM-FRIENDLY TIPS

In this example, we mention ableism. This is the prejudice, bias, or discrimination directed toward people living with disabilities. In our example, George has a diagnosis of DID, which is considered a disability under their insurance plan. We believe that multiplicity is simply a difference, and that diversity is an essential part of any working society. We do acknowledge, however, that living in a world that is designed for and run by singlets can be disabling for a vast majority, if not all, Systems.

Let's reflect on George and the impact Baz's actions had on him. As a reminder: After the conversation with George, Baz decided to talk with Carrie about how hurtful her comments are to George, and that she is ableist and should learn more about DID. Baz then texted George to let him know that he has told Carrie how hurtful she has been to him. George feels betrayed and that Baz is now an unsafe person to be around.

How would you describe the impact Baz's behavior has had on George?

_____

_____

_____

Let's think about it a little more deeply. George is clearly hurt by Baz's behavior. Could something else have contributed to the intensity of the impact, and if so, what? For example, the feeling of betrayal; the thought that Baz is an unsafe person.

_____

_____

_____

What about the decisions George has made? What do you think George believes were Baz's intentions? For example, *"Baz doesn't care about me at all. He just wants to create drama."*

_____

_____

_____

WORKSHEET 23 EXAMPLE

Here's what it may look like. As a reminder: George (System) was talking with Baz (singlet), his friend of three years.

George was discussing how hard it is for them to tell their other friend Carrie (singlet), a friend of one year, that she can sometimes make ableist comments. George told Baz that they understand Carrie doesn't mean to [doesn't intend to] be ableist but that it still hurts when they hear these statements, and they wish that Carrie would put more effort into learning about DID.

After that conversation, Baz decides to talk with Carrie about how hurtful her comments are to George, and that she is ableist and should learn more about DID. Baz then text-messages George, letting him know that he has told Carrie how hurtful she has been to him. George feels betrayed and that Baz is now an unsafe person to be around. To protect himself, George decides to block Baz on all social media and stops returning his text messages.

What do you think Baz's intentions are?

> *Baz intended to help George. He heard how hurt they were by Carrie's comments. Baz could see that George liked Carrie as a friend and wanted to be able to tell her about how they felt but was afraid to. Baz thought that if he told Carrie about it, he could resolve the conflict between everyone and that they would all be friendly again.*

What could Baz's conscious intentions be, and what might his subconscious intentions be?

> *Baz had past experiences where a childhood friend made hurtful comments to him about something he had no control over. He was afraid to talk to that friend and ended up not speaking to that friend ever again. He didn't realize he was still hurting about how that friendship had ended, and he felt shame about never having said anything, so he felt compelled to resolve it for George.*

How would you describe the impact Baz's behavior has had on George?

> *George was clearly hurt by Baz's behavior. George felt betrayed by Baz in his choice to talk to Carrie behind their back, without asking. George then felt that Baz could no longer be trusted with any of his feelings, because how could Baz not know that George would feel betrayed by his actions? Surely Baz would have known, and he still decided to do what he did, therefore making him an unsafe person. In order to protect themselves, George had no other option but to completely block Baz from all channels and end the friendship.*

Let's think about it a little more deeply. George is clearly hurt by Baz's behavior. Could something else have contributed to the intensity of the impact, and if so, what?

> *George has been hurt in the past by many people. George has talked to others about how they felt, including his sister. She went straight to their parents and told them how they felt. George had no idea she had done so, and only knew she had because their parents, the next week, were very angry and dismissive of their feelings. George felt betrayed by his sister, and some of his System vowed never to open up to anyone else again. On further reflection, George realized that one of his Littles was reexperiencing that feeling of betrayal, and that the Little's feelings contributed to the intensity of his hurt feelings.*

What about the decisions George has made? What do you think George believes were Baz's intentions? For example, *"Baz doesn't care about me at all. He just wants to create drama."*

> *George's actions reflected what they would have liked to be able to do with their sister all those years ago but couldn't. George made the decision that Baz was unsafe based on the intensity of their hurt. George believed that, like his sister's, Baz's actions would lead to intense anger and dismissal by Carrie. George wanted to avoid that potential outcome and decided to end the relationship with both Baz and Carrie.*

What could George have done instead of ending the relationship with two of their friends?

They may have been able to use the DEAR MAN strategy to explain to Baz how his actions impacted him. In that conversation, George may also have been able to set a boundary.

Next, let's have a look at setting boundaries.

SETTING BOUNDARIES

First, let's dispel some common myths about boundaries.

MYTHS

- If I make a request, this will show others I am weak, vulnerable, or can be taken advantage of.

- I have to know whether the other person will respect my boundary before I can set one.

- If the other person will say no, I shouldn't bother to set a boundary in the first place; there is no point.

- People will automatically do what I want, in the way I want, when I set a boundary.

- I only need to set a boundary once with people.

- If they don't respect my boundary after I tell them once, they clearly don't care.

- Boundaries are a guarantee that I'll get the outcome I want.

- Boundaries will push all the good people if my life away.

- In order to maintain my relationship with others, I can't set boundaries.

- If I don't have needs or squish them down, I don't have to set a boundary.

- If I set a boundary, people won't like me.

- People just know how to set boundaries.

- A boundary is a request for the person to change. I don't need to do anything after I communicate my boundary.

FACTS

- Boundaries are bridges. They are designed to build strong, healthy relationships with others.

- Boundaries are a request, not a demand, and involve two steps.

- Boundaries require a consequence of inaction to adhere to the spoken boundary (this is the second step).

- Boundaries are essential to having healthy, mature relationships.

- Setting boundaries and maintaining them is a learned skill that needs to be practiced—a lot.

- You 100 percent deserve to have your needs met, as do all humans.

- Boundaries need to be repeated, not because people don't care, but because they often forget when something new is put in place. People are often absorbed by their own worlds, not ours, and so need to be reminded.

- Boundaries are about you, not the other person. They are to show what you are willing to put up with and not willing to put up with.

- Without articulating your boundaries to others, resentment can build, and resentment can be a relationship killer.

- Boundaries need to be communicated. Other people cannot read our minds and respect unstated boundaries. Unstated boundaries lead to resentment and other unpleasant feelings.

TYPES OF BOUNDARIES

RIGID BOUNDARIES

These types of boundaries are closed and inflexible. They are like the impenetrable walls of a castle. These boundaries don't let anyone in or anything out. They isolate you from the outside world and from your internal world. They may look like demands instead of requests. There is no compromise with rigid boundaries.

OPEN BOUNDARIES

Open boundaries are unclear and likely too vague. This allows for other people to interpret what you want or need. Having too open or porous boundaries is akin to people-pleasing.

CLEAR AND HEALTHY BOUNDARIES

These are the kind we strive for. Clear boundaries are direct, specific, well-timed for both parties, and communicated with the intention to mend the relationship or build a stronger and healthier relationship.

PHYSICAL BOUNDARIES

These are the limits to your personal space and your preferred level of physical contact. This can include whether you prefer to stand a little farther away from others, prefer deep pressure hugs or none at all, or only want to high-five.

RESOURCE BOUNDARIES

Your resources are your finances, energy, time, and materials—your personal stuff. Setting a resource boundary can be as simple as saying *"I can't come to this week's D&D session. I need a rest week."* This is a time boundary and an energy-related boundary.

MENTAL OR EMOTIONAL BOUNDARIES

These types of boundaries are about respecting your own emotional needs and your limits, and they are designed to protect your emotional well-being. These boundaries also help in protecting how much you are willing and able to support another person. Without them, it may start to feel like you are their therapist. This can look like, *"Hey, I hear how overwhelmed you are about this. I'm not sure if I am the right person to help you right now. I've got a lot going on myself. Could we talk again in a few days?"*

WORKSHEET 24

Let's try to identify what your boundaries are for each type: physical, resource, mental, and emotional. What are your nonnegotiables? These are your deal-breakers or boundaries that you are not willing to compromise. Essentially, if crossed, the relationship ends.

What are our physical boundaries?

_____

_____

_____

_____

What are our resource boundaries?

_____

_____

_____

_____

What are our mental boundaries?

_____

_____

_____

What are our emotional boundaries?

_____

_____

_____

NONNEGOTIABLES

Nonnegotiables in any relationship with another person are the things that we will absolutely not compromise on, no matter what the situation or who the person is. We can also call these deal-breakers.

Not everyone has the same nonnegotiables, and that is OK. These are yours. You do not need to justify to anyone why these particular deal-breakers exist for you.

For example, your deal-breakers may be:

Illicit drugs and alcohol

It may be an absolute deal-breaker if the friend, partner, or new person in your life that you are trying to build a healthy relationship with misuses drugs or alcohol. It may also be a nonnegotiable if the person uses them at all.

Write below what your deal-breakers are. These are also considered red flags.

_____

_____

_____

_____

DEVELOPING INTERNAL RELATIONSHIPS

Interpersonal relationships are those developed with external folks. Accordingly, we call those developed with internal folks, your Headmates, *intrapersonal* relationships. The connections we develop with our Headmates are the most important for any System.

Developing relationships with your Headmates can also be described as System mapping. It can also include mapping the internal world itself. There are two types of System mapping: relational and topographic.

RELATIONAL MAPPING

Relational mapping is creating a visual diagram of how your Headmates are connected to each other. It assumes that all Headmates are equal in value and contribute to the System uniquely, and it is not based on a hierarchical structure. We can begin developing relationships with our Headmates through relational mapping, but first we need some identifying information about our Headmates: their role or job within the System.

Think of it as if you are developing an organizational chart for the System. Of course, this chart does not suggest that those who are higher in the chart are more important. We are simply mapping our role and relationship or connection to each other.

Let's begin by acknowledging that there are different types or roles of Headmates. We can say that each Headmate contributes to the System in different ways, based on their knowledge, experiences, attitudes, and beliefs.

HEADMATE ROLES AND TYPES

Below is a list of the types or roles each Headmate could have within your System. It's not an exhaustive list, of course. Read over the different types and roles that Headmates can have within a System. Do any resonate with you? Think about how each may contribute to your System.

Don't forget that there are more terms in the "Commonly Used Terms" section in the back of this book.

CARETAKER

A Headmate that looks after and supports the other System members is called the Caretaker. They can be for specific groups, like the Littles, or the System as a whole. This can look like emotional support or even physical support, for example, ensuring the Littles have somewhere they can feel secure internally.

GATEKEEPER

Gatekeepers are Headmates that have a level of influence over:

- who is fronting

- access to certain areas within the System

- access to other Headmates or even awareness of the existence of other Headmates

- information such as memories, or aspects of memories, emotions, and contextual information about the life, present or past

The Gatekeeper may front, have access to certain areas within the internal world, have access to certain memories or aspects of a memory, or may have access, connection, or awareness to other Headmates.

HOST

A Headmate who fronts the most and completes daily life is called the Host—like the host of a party. The Host can change over time, depending on a number of factors. The Host is not the "original alter," as there is no such thing as an original alter. All Headmates are equal and valid. The Host is just another role within the System.

PROTECTOR

A Headmate who protects the System in some way is the Protector. This can be from external stimulus, meaning protecting the body physically, or from internal stimulus, protecting other Headmates from specific information.

HOSTILE PROTECTOR

Also known as a Persecutor in the clinical realm, the Hostile Protector is our Headmate who protects the System using hostile, aggressive, or destructive means. This could be by canceling your therapy appointments, harassing other Headmates, or other more intense behaviors.

Technically, you can consider every Headmate within your System a protector. Each in their own way is protecting from things either externally or internally. For example, the Gatekeeper protects information, and the Host protects others from having to engage in day-to-day life.

SYSTEM-FRIENDLY TIPS

It is important that we remember that all your Headmates are doing the best they can to cope, using strategies they've learned over time and from their experiences. There is no such thing as a bad Headmate. Try your best to be nonjudgmental of how each Headmate currently copes. That is what therapy is for: to learn new, healthier ways to cope.

WORKSHEET 25

Using the above roles and types of Headmates, let's start to reflect on how each of you contributes to the System in your own unique way. To simplify, try completing the prompt below, for each Headmate that wants to engage in this activity.

I protect the System by …

_____

_____

_____

_____

_____

_____

_____

_____

_____

_____

_____

_____

WORKSHEET 25 EXAMPLE

Using the above roles and types of Headmates, let's start to reflect on how each of you contributes to the System in your own unique way. To simplify, try completing the prompt below, for each Headmate that wants to engage in this activity.

I protect the System by …

Wendy: *I protect the System by keeping the Littles away from front when we are on public transportation.*

Don: *I protect the System by fronting when we are around dangerous people who could hurt the body.*

Wren: *I protect the System by holding onto some memories that no one else is allowed to know about.*

Truth: *I protect the System by detecting whether we are being lied to or manipulated.*

SS: *We protect the System by keeping things hidden. Do not ask us what. You are not allowed to know.*

WORKSHEET 26

We can now use this information to create a relational map. It can look however you want it to. Here is an example.

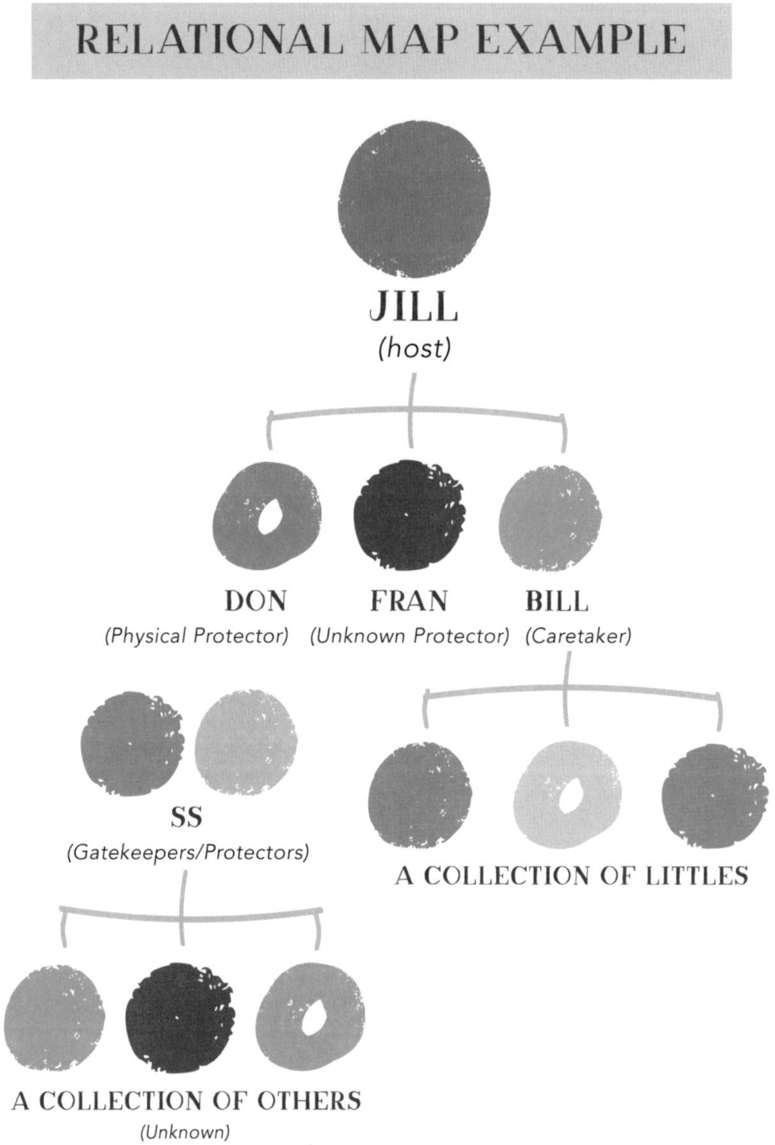

Figure 5.1. Example relational map

SYSTEM-FRIENDLY TIPS

This example shows Jill at the top of the relational map. However, think of it as Jill being at the front of the map. Jill in this example is the Host—her position is at the front of the Headspace, with the other Headmates farther inside.

BUILDING RELATIONSHIPS

Other ways you can start to build relationships with your internal family can include:

Developing a list of things you like. Include things like colors, flavors, textures, or TV shows and movies. Once you have a list, you can invite those inside to come close to the front to enjoy these things. For example, Don likes to watch the TV show *Rick and Morty*. Others could put the show on and invite Don to come and watch it together. Consider this parallel play: playing adjacent to each other but not trying to influence one another's behavior.

Inviting others inside to take part in pleasant activities. This could be as simple as sending out an internal invite, thinking aloud in your head: *"Anyone who wants to come and take part in X, you are welcome to join."* X could be a nice warm cup of tea, sitting and watching the clouds go by, or eating chicken nuggets together.

Connecting with your Headmates does not have to be complicated or scary. It will take time for you all to meet each other and to become familiar with each other.

SYSTEM-FRIENDLY TIPS

There is no specific formula when it comes to connecting with your Headmates. It's normal for some Systems to take years of practice to build their relationships.

CREATE A MEETING PLACE

When developing relationships with your Headmates, it can be helpful to have a neutral place to meet, where formal introductions can occur or where others can feel things out with you.

Try imagining a place where you would feel comfortable meeting someone new. This could be a reading nook at a library or a private garden. This place will be your meeting place. It may be near the front and accessible to those who front as well as those farther back in the Headspace. This is a place where you can invite those you've met in therapy to talk more together.

Not all Systems experience their internal world in a visual way. Some only experience feelings or emotions. Some experience a sense of things. There is no right way or wrong way to experience your internal world.

SYSTEM-FRIENDLY TIPS

It is generally unhelpful to go looking or searching for new Head-mates to meet, especially if you are not supported by a counselor or therapist. You never know who you are going to meet and what they may hold. Ideally, you let the System naturally unfold and make itself known as opposed to making things go faster by undertaking an exploratory adventure internally.

If your meeting place is visual, try drawing it here. Use as much color and detail as you like. This can be an opportunity for the Littles to be creative. You can also use pictures from books or magazines and create a collage of what you'd like your meeting place to look or feel like.

SYSTEM-FRIENDLY TIPS

Much like searching for new Headmates, exploring the internal world without support may lead to uncovering things you may not be ready for. We encourage you to go slow and engage with supports if you choose to explore the internal world.

TOPOGRAPHIC MAPPING

If you feel comfortable to try mapping the internal world, going an extra step beyond creating a meeting place, you can draw it here. An example is in figure 5.2 on the next page, where you can also color in.

Figure 5.2.

NEED A COLORING BREAK?

Surviving the Moment Skills

- Body-Based Strategies Versus Brain-Based Strategies
- Getting Through a Moment of Crisis

BODY-BASED STRATEGIES VERSUS BRAIN-BASED STRATEGIES

BRAIN-BASED STRATEGIES

Brain-based strategies are those that acknowledge your capacity to engage with your frontal lobe, the part of the brain that is involved with higher executive functions. This is a fancy way of referring to complex mental skills such as decision-making and problem-solving, regulating emotions, planning and organizing, impulse control, and more. When we are in a moment of crisis, it is unlikely that the frontal lobe is online, so it is unfair to expect someone in crisis to engage in brain-based strategies that require the frontal lobe.

Some of the brain-based strategies included in this workbook are those within the "People and Parts Relationship Skills" module, the "Values-Guided Action Skills" module, and some of the skills in the "Managing Our Emotions Skills" module.

BODY-BASED STRATEGIES

Our body-based approach focuses on the physical body and the physiological experiences as the starting point for processing large amounts of information when you and your System are in a moment of crisis. When we talk about information here, we are referring to your thoughts, emotions, and body sensations experienced in a moment of crisis.

EXAMPLES OF STRATEGIES

Jill is the Host of their System. They are currently in a moment of crisis and having lots of thoughts whirling around in the Headspace. Jill is struggling to make sense of any of their thoughts. She tries to focus on one, but they feel like they just slip through her fingers. Jill is noticing that others inside are screaming and likely in some kind of flashback. Jill feels the body tensing up and the heart beating fast. Jill has limited communication with others in the back of the Headspace.

In this example, the System is likely in a fight-or-flight state and hyper-aroused. The idea of asking Jill to calm down and use thinking-based strategies like Think Purple seems unrealistic and like setting them up for failure—so we don't expect them to. No one can be expected to engage in thinking-based strategies when they can't think.

You can use body-based strategies, designed to help shift you out of the immediate moment of crisis, avoid thoughts of PAILED (permanent and irreversible life-ending decisions), and enter a Headspace where you and other Headmates have actual capacity to engage with brain-based strategies.

Some Systems are only able to engage in body-based strategies to begin with. Some may be only able to engage in brain-based strategies some of the time, and some can use both at any time. You are not expected to be able to do something you aren't able to do, given where you currently are on your journey of healing. We also acknowledge that there is the System journey, your journey as a team, and then there is *your* journey, as a Headmate within the System. All are valid.

SYSTEM-FRIENDLY TIPS

In this workbook we use the term PAILED, pronounced like "bailed," which stands for "permanent and irreversible life-ending decisions," instead of the word *suicide*.

BODY BASED STRATEGIES

I can hear some of you say, "WTF! I don't want to connect with the body; it's an unsafe place to be." That is totally understandable. We aren't necessarily asking you to connect with the body in this module. This workbook is designed for Systems who have experienced, well, what you've experienced. In the following module, we are working on trying to survive the moment of crisis. Here's what we think it may feel like we are asking, when you are asked to connect with the body:

> "Slow down and start to focus on your body parts. Really tune into the sensations of those body parts. Don't get triggered or you've done it wrong. While you are connecting with the body, you will start to feel relief, calm, and all the unpleasantness will fade away, and you'll feel OK. If you don't, then it isn't working—you aren't focusing properly, or focusing enough."

Here's what we are actually trying to say:

> "We know you are in a moment of crisis that feels like it may never end, that feels so intense and all-consuming that thoughts of PAILED may sound like the only option. Your frontal lobe, the thinking part of your brain, the rational decision-maker, is offline. We know you can't think your way out of this moment of crisis. Let's use strategies that don't involve thinking and that redirect your efforts to shifting the body—essentially your nervous system—out of this threat response so that you *can* be in a space to then use brain-based strategies."

GETTING THROUGH A MOMENT OF CRISIS

WHAT IS A CRISIS?

This workbook is not for times when you are actively considering suicide. That requires immediate action with a mental health professional. If you are currently in immediate danger, call the emergency services in your region—you deserve to be safe. Dial 988 in the United States and Canada, 000 in Australia, or 999 in Britain.

When we discuss the idea of suicide in this section, we differentiate between passive thoughts and active thoughts. Passive thoughts of this nature are just that—thoughts about it, not beyond that. Again, this workbook is not designed for anyone currently experiencing active thoughts of suicide. We use the term PAILED to be a little less confronting.

So how do we define *crisis* for the purposes of this workbook, adapting it for the experience of multiplicity? We can consider a crisis to be:

- **A temporary situation.** We acknowledge that all moments pass. Change is inevitable and guaranteed.

- **A situation where you feel awful.** The feelings are specifically related to emotional and psychological pain. As discussed in the "Pain, Damage, Illness" section in the Grounding Skills module, we acknowledge that as a System you can experience different types of pain. For this module, we consider somatic flashbacks, or past pain that is experienced in the here and now, as emotional and psychological pain.

- **A risky situation.** This is a situation where you or anyone else within you System is at risk of acting in a way that creates damage or illness to the body or involves thoughts of PAILED.

SYSTEM-FRIENDLY TIPS

We acknowledge that some of your Headmates may act on thoughts of PAILED without you or other Headmates knowing. This can be confronting and scary. You are not expected to know where others inside are on their journey of healing.

HECAAS

The acronym HECAAs is pronounced "heckers," Australian slang for "hectic." It stands for:

Halt. Before doing anything right now, halt and do nothing. This includes physical movement, activities, and tasks. Halting is our first step when we recognize that we are in a moment of crisis. By halting, we give ourselves an extra moment before acting. Essentially, we are trying to avoid impulsive actions.

Ease off. Where possible, ease off your engagement with whatever the situation is. If you can, remove yourself altogether from the situation. If this is not an option, easing off can mean creating some distance between you and the situation. This can be as simple as taking a long breath in and out or saying out loud, "I think we are in a moment of crisis. Let's ease off what we are doing." By saying this out loud, it literally takes a moment, which is easing off.

Collect. Once you've halted and eased off as much as you can, use Logic Mind, from the "Thinking Purple" section of the Managing Your Emotions Skills module. Invite your Headmates who are observers, rational, or logic-oriented to come as close to front as possible. Ask those Headmates to help you collect data about the situation. What is occurring within the environment? Is it completely overstimulating? Is there a trigger around that you weren't aware of before? Are there any thoughts or emotions occurring that can be noted? Again, we are simply collecting the data.

Act in Alignment. Our last step is consolidating the data collected and make a conscious choice to act in alignment of your System's values. You can use the Difficult Emotions Decision Tree, figure 3.2 in the "Managing Our Emotions Skills" module, to assist in the decision-making.

SYSTEM-FRIENDLY TIPS

We acknowledge that in a moment of crisis, it can be really challenging to think clearly and make decisions that are in line with your System's values and keep you safe. Using the Difficult Emotions Decision Tree (figure 3.2) can help take some of that cognitive load off your plate.

ALTERING HOW YOUR BODY FEELS

You can use strategies that involve less thinking and reflecting and more doing. By altering how your body feels, your focus is purely on the nervous system as a way to assist getting closer to your Window of Tolerance.

In a moment of crisis you and your Headmates are likely in a fight-or-flight state. As discussed in the Window of Tolerance section at the beginning of this workbook, in a fight-or-flight state or hyperarousal, your body can experience the following:

- racing heart rate

- tunnel vision, or vision becoming sharper

- tense muscles

When your body is experiencing this, you may also have lots of unpleasant racing thoughts as well as intense and overwhelming emotions, and you may go in and out of flashbacks. While it would be wonderful to talk or logic your way out of it, that's not realistic. In this state your frontal lobe is not online. What *can* you do? You can use a body-based approach.

TEMPERATURE

Using temperature can be an effective and immediate strategy to influence how you feel in your body. In a moment of crisis, you can use cold water or an ice pack to, in a way, shock your body. The cold puts the body into a dive reflex, an evolutionary adaptation for survival. How does this apply to you?

In a moment of crisis, your body may respond as if a threat has been detected and rapidly activate your energy resources, increase your heart rate, raise your blood pressure, and redirect blood flow to the muscles. All this is to assist the fight-or-flight response. With a racing heart and blood flowing to your muscles, you can run as fast as possible away from the threat, or punch and kick the threat with all the energy you have in your body.

Your body is responding to a moment of crisis in the same way it would to a giant bear looming in front of you, even though that is not a likely threat in the here and now. Activating the dive reflex through the simple use of cold water or an ice pack on the back of your neck leads to an immediate reduction in your heart rate, allowing you a window of opportunity to make the next decision in line with your values and staying safe.

SYSTEM-FRIENDLY TIPS

This strategy can be very effective and is simple to do. It is important to be aware of any heart-related issues, as the rapid reduction in heart rate may not be medically safe. Check with your physician if you are unsure.

Also, be mindful that for some Systems, the use of sudden and intense cold may in fact do the opposite of what you are trying to achieve. If for any reason you believe the use of this strategy may trigger trauma memories, don't engage with this strategy.

DISSOCIATION AND DISTRACTION

In a moment of crisis, the use of dissociation and distraction may be helpful to get through it. Yes, you heard that right: using dissociation may be helpful. In the words of the wise Dr. Jamie Marich, dissociation is not a dirty word.

As a System, you are an expert in dissociating. Why not use it when you are in a moment of crisis? Here, we are suggesting the use of dissociation as a functional strategy to get through a moment of crisis. What might functional dissociation actually look like? Something specific and personalized to you and your System would require a conversation with your therapist or counselor, but we can discuss it in general terms.

FUNCTIONAL DISSOCIATION

- Asking another Headmate to come front and ensure that the body is safe, for example, calling on a Caretaker or Protector. This may assist in allowing the moment to pass and avoid acting on PAILED.

- Dampening your connection to your emotions may also assist in getting through the moment so that you can avoid acting on PAILED. You may ask a Gatekeeper or Protector to reduce the noise in your emotional experience in that moment of crisis.

SYSTEM-FRIENDLY TIPS

Remember, PAILED stands for "permanent and irreversible life-ending decision." Asking another Headmate to come and take over front so that you don't act on thoughts of PAILED is a way to keep safe. Building on this with your therapist or counselor is then the next stage of your healing journey.

DISTRACTION

What about using distraction as another option for getting through the moment of crisis? "Distraction" is a fancy way of saying functional avoidance. Again, avoidance isn't bad in this context, as your aim is simply to get through the moment to the point where the moment of crisis has passed. Some options can include:

- Focus all your attention on a task you need to get done, like washing the dishes.
- Put on your favorite movie or TV show, even if you only need to watch twenty minutes of it to get through the moment of crisis.
- Jump on the computer and play your favorite game: zone in to another world.
- Do some exercise: moving the body may help shift you into a different mind-set.
- Grab your favorite comfort snack.
- Reflect on your System values and engage in a task that honors them.
- Call or message a friend.
- Compare how you are feeling now to a time when you felt different and less unpleasant.
- Scroll through social media.
- Listen to a song that you can loudly sing all the words to.
- If you're religious or spiritual, pray or engage in a meaningful spiritual practice.
- Totally deny the problem for the moment—until the moment of crisis passes.
- Color in—there are some coloring options in this workbook.

- Listen to very loud music so you can't hear your own thoughts or the internal noise.

- Hold ice in your hand for as long as you can. Time yourself and try to beat the time.

- List other things that your System has used that works in distracting you:

_____

_____

_____

_____

Reflection Time

HOW DID IT GO?

WORKSHEET 27

Think about what sections in this book have worked well for you and your System. What about them worked well?

_____

_____

_____

_____

_____

_____

_____

At this point, think about what sections in this book you decided to skip, or those that didn't work well for you. What about them were you not ready for, or what didn't work well?

_____

_____

_____

_____

_____

_____

_____

FUTURE GOALS

WORKSHEET 28

Now think about what future goals you'd like to set for yourself and your System. Where would you like to see yourselves, as a team, in one, three, and six months' time?

_____

_____

_____

_____

_____

_____

_____

_____

_____

_____

_____

_____

_____

Extra Notes

Extra Doodling Space

Commonly Used Terms

Age Slider, Age Sliding: A Headmate whose age changes or slides, or who identifies as being different ages at different times. This can sometimes be called regression, but Age Sliders can become younger or older. All Headmates, including Hosts, can age-slide.

alter: The clinical term for an individual in a System. *Alter* is a shorter version of "an alternate state of consciousness," typically used in the literature. Within this workbook, we have used the term *Headmate* instead of *alter*. Alternatively, the word *part* can also be used.

Big: Adults in the System. It is important to understand the cognitive and emotional capacity of each Headmate, not just their age.

blurring or blendy: When two or more Headmates are fronting and the line or boundaries between them gets blurred. This can occur for different reasons, such as when there is poor communication between Headmates, or no knowledge of being multiple. It can also occur in times of stress, when the System finds it challenging to find clarity in their individuality. This can also be an ongoing process for Systems who are less separate, or fit more with OSDD (other specified dissociative disorder) versus DID.

Caretaker: A Headmate that looks after the others internally. This can be for specific groups, like the Littles, or the entire System.

Co-conscious or co-con: When two or more Headmates are conscious at the same time. A Headmate can be farther to the front and have greater influence over body movement, speech, and so on while a second Headmate can have influence over thought, memory-sharing, and emotional experiences. For example, two Headmates stand together, one in front and one behind the other, but both are in the front space. Headmates can experience blurring while being co-con.

Co-fronting: When two or more Headmates have influence over the body's function at once. It is similar to being co-con but with more even or equal influence between each Headmate. For example, two Headmates stand next to each other in the front.

Co-Host: Backup or secondary Hosts. Not all Systems have just one Headmate completing the role of Host; every System is different.

companion: System mates that exist to keep other Headmates company. These can be human and nonhuman, for example, a cat companion.

dormancy: When a Headmate "falls asleep" for an extended period of time. This typically means there is no contact with others within the internal Headspace. Headmates cannot cease to exist, but they can remain dormant for weeks, months, or years. This can be the choice of a Headmate should they have the capacity or skill to place themselves in dormancy. Headmates can also be placed in dormancy by others within the System. Dormancy can create a sense of grief and loss for those within the System.

down the System, downing the System: An internal or external trigger to the System that creates a shutdown response to one or more of the Headmates, and likely most of them. This may lead to rapid switching or appearing catatonic to an external observer.

factive: Headmates based on real people, living or deceased; for example, a Headmate based on Henry Cavill, the actor who played Superman. They can also be based on real people from the System's life, like a perpetrator. A factive falls under the umbrella term of *Introject*.

fictive: Headmates based on fictitious characters like those in movies or books; for example, a Headmate based on Superman. A fictive also falls under the umbrella term of *Introject*.

fronting: When a Headmate has control over the body. Anytime a Headmate is fronting, they will have some level of control over the body's actions: facial expressions, use of the voice, movements of the arms and legs, and so on. The front space is the place where Headmates are when they are fronting, also described as being up front.

front Stuck: When a Headmate is unable to stop fronting or is forced to keep control of the body. Typically the Headmate can't leave the front at all. This can be the choice of the Headmate fronting or from someone else within the System at the displeasure of the front stuck Headmate.

Fusion: When two or more Headmates fuse to become one Headmate for an amount of time. It can be permanent or time-limited. When Fusion is forced or occurs unnaturally, it will typically fall apart. This may lead to the experience of grief and loss as two Headmates merge to become a third, new Headmate. Think of Fusion as combining two paint colors. Yellow and blue fused together make green. Within green still lives both yellow and blue.

Gatekeeper: A Headmate that has a level of control over:

- who is fronting
- access to certain areas within the System
- access to other Headmates or even awareness of the existence of other Headmates
- information such as memories or aspects of memories, emotions, and contextual information about the life, present or past

Headspace, inner world, internal world: Where the Headmates exist, inside the mind. This environment, unlike the external world, can be infinite in its creation and capacity. For example, the rules of gravity and time do not exist in the internal world in the same way they do in the external world. Not all Systems will have knowledge of their internal world or access to it.

Host: The Headmate who fronts the most and performs the typical daily activities. The Host is not considered the original Headmate; it is a misconception that there is an original. The term *Host* describes the role or function of a Headmate and is not tied permanently to one specific Headmate, as the Host can change over time. It is important that your therapist understands this and works with all of you, not just the current Host.

Integration: When the walls of amnesia between Headmates begin to fade, disappear, or become more transparent. Often Integration and Fusion are used synonymously, but they describe different processes. Integration is part of the healing and recovery process as it involves building trusting relationships between Headmates.

Introject: A Headmate that is partly based on an outside source or fully embodies an outside source. It identifies as the source itself: for example, the Headmate identifies as Superman or Henry Cavill. There are a number of different types of Introjects, including fictives and factives.

Little: Young children in a System. These are highly vulnerable Headmates and should be treated age-appropriately.

multiplicity: The state of being plural or multiple.

outer world, external world: The opposite of the Headspace; the world where the body itself exists, where the limits of gravity, time, and so on exist.

Persecutor: A Headmate that copes using destructive or harmful strategies, such as harming the physical body. Usually, these Headmates hold internalized abuse narratives, using maladaptive or old strategies to protect the System. Persecutory Headmates can also be Introjects. In this workbook we refer to these Headmates as *Hostile Protectors* to acknowledge the intent of their actions.

Protector: Every Headmate within a System can be considered a Protector. Each Headmate protects themselves and the System in different ways: some healthy and adaptive, some unhealthy and harmful.

rapid switching: A process where multiple Headmates can be cycled through the front space. This may be because lots of Headmates want to be fronting at once, or no one wants to front at all. This typically occurs when the System is in distress or triggered.

singlet, singelton: A non-System.

singletsona: The mask that the System uses to feign singlet status. Much like autistic masking, a singletsona is used to protect the System, where whomever is fronting acts as if they are a singlet.

splitting: When a Headmate separates into two or more Headmates. This is a functional process within a System. For example, if one Headmate cannot manage the intensity of some memories, that Headmate may split, creating two Headmates—one to hold the factual information and one to hold the emotional information. Splitting can occur during times of trauma or intense distress, when the System does not have the necessary coping skills to manage the distressing situation.

switching: When Headmates in a System change who is fronting. This may cause headaches and sometimes nausea or other physically unpleasant symptoms for those coming into the front space.

System: The collection of Headmates inside the physical body. It can also be called a collective, or used with another word prior to describe everyone, for example, the Multiverse System.

System Admin: Headmates that help keep the System organized. They may keep track of Headmates, medications, appointments, and so on. They may also keep track of internal workings, like a librarian.

Trauma Holder: A Headmate that holds traumatic experiences. Any Headmate can be a Trauma Holder. These experiences may be held in pieces, where one Headmates holds on to the somatic information of the traumatic experience and another Headmate holds on to the emotional information.

SYSTEM-FRIENDLY TIPS

Persecutors deserve acceptance, validation, and respect, like every other Headmate. It is important to remember that they are not bad or evil. They are often Headmates in extreme pain and believe that they should not exist because they harm the System. It can be helpful in treatment to teach Persecutors more constructive, functional coping strategies.

SCAN TO DOWNLOAD DID EMERGENCY CARD

ACKNOWLEDGMENTS

To my clients—past, present, and future—who have inspired this workbook. Thank you for trusting me to bear witness to your healing journeys. Your courage and resilience continue to shape and inspire my work. A heartfelt thank you to North Atlantic Books for believing in this project and taking a chance on me. Your support has made this workbook a reality. A special mention to Dr. Jamie Marich, whose kind words and belief in this project gave me the encouragement I needed. And finally, to my past self—for always having the courage to believe that I could make a difference in this world.

ABOUT THE AUTHOR

Photo by Andy at www.athousandmilesphotography.com.au

Johanna Knyn is a dedicated psychologist with a passion for guiding individuals through their healing journey. Her area of expertise is in dissociative identity disorder (DID). As the founder of Guided Healing Psychology, her private practice serves as a safe haven for clients navigating the complexities of DID.

In addition to her clinical work, Johanna is an advocate for education and awareness surrounding DID. Her commitment to dispelling myths and fostering a System-affirming approach has led her to present at conferences, where she shares her expertise with colleagues in the field. Recognizing the importance of supporting university students and staff, Johanna has provided bespoke training and workshops to enhance understanding and create a more inclusive environment for individuals with DID.

Johanna's commitment to bridging the gap between academia and practical application is evident in her self-published works. She has authored an insightful ebook tailored for clinicians entering the field of DID and an introductory document for colleagues new to working with this complex disorder. Taking a step further, Johanna has also written a children's book titled *My Mommy Has Multiple Parts,* offering a child-friendly and affirming way for parents with DID to explain their condition to their children. Her work aims to provide representation in mainstream media, fostering understanding and empathy.

As a singlet—someone without DID—Johanna emphasizes the importance of including the voices of those with lived experience in the development of therapeutic materials. She actively engages with those with DID, recognizing the necessity of collaboration to create more effective and inclusive resources for healing. Johanna Knyn stands as an example of how compassion, expertise, and dedication can break down barriers and promote understanding in the field of psychology.

ABOUT NORTH ATLANTIC BOOKS

North Atlantic Books (NAB) is an independent, nonprofit publisher committed to a bold exploration of the relationships between mind, body, spirit, and nature. Founded in 1974, NAB aims to nurture a holistic view of the arts, sciences, humanities, and healing. To make a donation or to learn more about our books, authors, events, and newsletter, please visit www.northatlanticbooks.com.